RIGHTEOUS BUSINESS

30 DAYS

TO

BETTER

BUSINESS

PRACTICE

ADAM MALLETT, JR.

WESTBOW
P R E S S®
A DIVISION OF THOMAS NELSON
& ZONDERVAN

WestBow Press books may be ordered through booksellers or by contacting:

WestBow Press
A Division of Thomas Nelson & Zondervan
1663 Liberty Drive
Bloomington, IN 47403
www.westbowpress.com
844-714-3454

Scripture quotations are taken from The Holy Bible, English Standard Version® (ESV®), Copyright © 2001 by Crossway, a publishing ministry of Good News Publishers. All rights reserved.

ISBN: 978-1-6642-5005-5 (sc)
ISBN: 978-1-6642-5004-8 (hc)
ISBN: 978-1-6642-5006-2 (e)

Library of Congress Control Number: 2021923386

Print information available on the last page.

WestBow Press rev. date: 12/28/2021

Dedicated to Frank Walker
"Excelsior"

CONTENTS

Introduction ix

Discipline: Continual Development 1

Favor: The Lord's Work 7

Integrity: The Key To Lasting Success 13

Assistance: Always Have A Partner 19

Perspective: Your Thoughts Determine Everything 25

Speak Wisely: What You Say Or Don't Say 31

Longevity: Long-Term Focus 37

Commendation: Good Business Practice And Recognition 43

Honesty: Define Your Success 49

Respect: Appreciating Your Business...................................... 55

Vision: Clear Vision And Consistent Effort............................61

Contentment: Focus On Your Own Results............................67

Speak Your Heart: Speech Reveals Character........................ 73

Fulfillment: Find Fulfillment In The Fruits Of Your Work............. 79

Counsel: Seek Expert Advice 85

Patience: Receive Feedback With Grace 91

Feedback: Consistently Communicate With Peers 97

Reservation: Slow To Speak, Quick To Encourage.......................... 103

Truthfulness: Even When It Hurts, Honesty Is Good Business... 107

Planning: Fail To Plan, Plan To Fail 113

Failures: Setbacks Are Not Failures 119

Actions: Act The Truth 123

Acumen: Expertise Requires Constant Growth 129

Leadership: Diligence Develops Leaders 135

Anxiety: Hear A Good Word, Speak A Good Word 141

Neighboring: Be A Good Neighbor 147

Resources: Every Resource Is A Blessing 153

Righteousness: Righteous Business Requires Righteous
Living 159

Conclusion 165

Bibliography 167

INTRODUCTION

Righteous Business is the kind of business that we all should practice. As I studied Proverbs 12 during the last year of my Christian Leadership and Management coursework at Regent University, I was convicted by Proverbs 12:27. "Whoever is slothful will not roast his game, but the diligent man will get precious wealth." Whatever resources I have available to me are blessings from God, intended to be used as efficiently and productively as possible. Any time, talent, or treasure that I neglect to use, or use wastefully, is an affront to the One who blessed me. As I meditated on this verse, I read the entire chapter over again, and the Holy Spirit convicted me with the wisdom on good business practice contained in every verse. I started jotting down notes of what each verse had to say about righteous business, and quickly realized that there was more than what I could fit in my morning Bible study time. That conviction has developed into the devotional that you are now reading. Whether you are an entrepreneur, a manager or supervisor, an hourly employee, or even a stay-at-home parent, the wisdom in Proverbs 12 is applicable for improving work ethic, diligence, and leadership in everyone.

For pastors, this book is especially challenging. The pastor's role in his church is not different from that of the manager of a business. We hate to think of our church as a business, but it operates just like any other organization. It consists of teams of people who perform different tasks, all working towards the same common goal. A pastor is a leader and manager. In the case of the church-planter, a pastor is also an entrepreneur. I would encourage every pastor who reads this book to view themselves as a manager just as much as they are a leader. We are leading people who are on fire for the Gospel, but we cannot do so without managing our resources well. Passion for the work of the Kingdom should be coupled with diligence, structure, and order in conducting that work.

Thank you for choosing to read this book. It is my prayer that this will be an encouragement to everyone who reads it. I would ask that you read this book as though it were a one-month devotional, reading a chapter a day. There are 28 chapters, along with this introduction and a conclusion. I would encourage you to read, study, and meditate on all of Proverbs 12 today, before you read the first chapter of the book. Despite being a book about business, work ethic, and leadership, this is, at its heart, an exegetical study of a chapter of God's Word. I will exclusively be referencing the English Standard Version of the Bible throughout this book; however, if you prefer a different translation, feel free to use it, as the wisdom of God stands above my own preference in translation. I am quite far from being an expert theologian, but I believe that God has used me to share at least some key wisdom with you, so that you might be edified.

DISCIPLINE: CONTINUAL DEVELOPMENT

Proverbs 12:1

"Whoever loves discipline loves knowledge,
but he who hates reproof is stupid"

T hough this book is a study of Proverbs 12, I would like to start by pointing your attention to Proverbs 5:23: "He dies for lack of discipline." If there were a top-five list of important attributes for successfully navigating life, discipline makes the list. I would even argue that if the Bible says a person dies without discipline, so also does a person's business die without discipline. Discipline is the foundation of what it means to build success. Though chapter 9 will discuss in detail what it means to define success for yourself and your business, understand that success is defined by what God says is good, right, and productive. Whatever you do, do it with discipline, or you will see it fail.

Discipline is a word that most people cringe or scoff at. Discipline is hard, uncomfortable, and unnatural. However, if we understand the implications of what it means to be disciplined, our approach to being disciplined will become much more natural. The word *discipline* looks quite like the word *disciple*. I am not a linguist, but I would say that these two words look similar. A disciple is someone who follows someone or someone's example. In the Bible, we see Jesus's disciples as those who followed Him during His earthly ministry. But even after He died, they were still His disciples. We can then understand that a disciple is someone who follows the example, teachings, and leadership of someone else. This is where the disconnect happens for us in being excited about being disciplined. We are naturally willing to follow a good leader, but we struggle with finding a leader who is genuinely good! Whenever a good leader is not present, we default to the next best leader. Often, this means following poor examples, which leads to poor discipline.

Many of us who try to become more disciplined are unsure of what example we are trying to follow. Maybe if you are trying to be more disciplined in exercising or eating right, you follow the example of your friend who is obsessed with CrossFit. Are you obsessed with CrossFit? If not, you will fail at being disciplined in that area. Or you will become obsessed with CrossFit. Are you trying to be more disciplined in studying the Bible? You might choose to follow the example of your favorite apologist or evangelist. However, if you were to find out that they had a secret stronghold of sin, would that shake your ability to be disciplined? Discipline, if it will be long-lasting and maximally effective in our lives, must follow the best example possible!

We ought to look to the Word of God as our foundation for our discipline. John 1 tells us that Jesus is the Living Word of God. By following the example of Jesus and faithfully studying His Word, we can be truly disciplined in every aspect of our lives. Jesus never owned His own business, but even He understood excellent business discipline.

> "For which of you, desiring to build a tower,
> does not first sit down and count the cost,
> whether he has enough to complete it?"
> Luke 14:28

Jesus used a business analogy to discuss the cost of discipleship with those who desired to follow Him. Using this as a context for Proverbs 12:1, we can see that understanding our businesses is a key part of being able to be disciplined in business. If we desire to be disciplined, we must love knowledge! Whatever business we are in, we must understand that business, that industry. If I want to open a successful restaurant, I must not only have an excellent work ethic and attitude, but I must also understand the restaurant industry! This is what Jesus was referring to when He said that someone desiring to build a tower must count the cost. To count the cost, the builder must understand the business of building towers. Not even the hardest working person could build a thriving, long-lasting business in an industry about which they fail to learn.

For those of you starting your own business or starting a new career, do not let this discourage you! We are all ignorant about many things. You do not know what you do not know. However, being disciplined means being committed to learning everything that you need to learn! Jesus expected His disciples to learn more about the Bible as they followed Him, even though He was the Living Word of God incarnate. We all must start somewhere in our journey toward being disciplined people, and we all must start somewhere in our careers. Start with discipline. Start with being a disciple of what the Bible says about arduous work, right morals, and success. Then be a disciple of the business in which you work. A truly disciplined businessperson is always becoming more of an expert in their field. This requires determination, but you can do it!

What business am I in?

Am I a disciplined person?

What one step can I take today to become more disciplined?

Am I willing to repeat that step tomorrow?

FAVOR:
THE LORD'S WORK

Proverbs 12:2

"A good man obtains favor from the Lord,
but a man of evil devices he condemns."

Favor is something that is very misunderstood among most people. Especially in business, favor and blessings are not seen as being key to any amount of success. I must confess that in every business I have worked, I have put my own knowledge, skill, and effort above any kind of favor or blessing. Throughout this book, we will discuss business expertise and work ethic more than we will discuss blessings or favor, but please do not neglect to remember the impact that the favor and blessings of God have on the success of our businesses!

Luke 2:52 tells us, at an early point in Jesus's life, that Jesus was growing in favor with God. This is important to keep in mind as we consider the content of both this book and the gospel stories. Everything that Jesus did while on earth was because He was in favor with God. Jesus *was* God, yet while on earth, He made it clear that He only did what the Father led Him to do. Because He was in favor with God, He knew the best steps to take and the best things to say. Because He was in favor with God, He could be in favor with those who followed Him. This is our model to emulate as we seek to make the right business moves.

Having the favor of God refers not to being owed something special or extra, but to receiving acceptance or blessings. When we read the word *favor* in the Bible, whether in the New Testament or the Old Testament, we are reading a translation of a word that is also often translated as "grace" or "mercy." With this understanding, we can see that having the favor of God is something more foundational than just extra blessings sprinkled on top of whatever we already have going for us in life. In the same way that we cannot even have true life without mercy and grace, so also can we not have true success without mercy and grace. Without the favor of the Lord, we may find some measure of success, but that success will be limited to our time here on earth.

This may be a difficult concept to let sink into our hearts and minds, for we can see businesses with multigenerational success, despite not being run by Christians. I would offer two considerations, both important to understanding the heart of what this book is trying to impress upon you. First, even those who are not children of God can follow biblical principles. The most "unsaved" person in the world can still have good morals and shrewd business practice. These people, though destined to spend eternity apart from God, will still find themselves blessed in accordance with the promises of the Word of God. They may have blessed business without having ever received the greatest blessing of new life in Christ.

Second, even the most successful business can still fall short of success as defined by God. A family may maintain a successful business for many generations, but even all those lifetimes put together are still a vapor compared with eternity. Regardless of your businesses, you ought to be able to define the eternal impact that you and your businesses can have. If you are in a business that has no apparent way of having an eternal impact on people and on creation, you may need to reexamine yourself and your businesses. Either you lack the godly wisdom to cast that eternal vision, or your businesses is simply one that is not eternally significant. Even a retail store has the eternal impact of providing people with the basic resources that they need to share the gospel, feed the hungry, clothe the poor, and so on.

Now that we understand what favor is and is not, we must understand how it applies to our lives and our businesses. Hopefully, you are already gaining some idea of that. Scripture is filled with examples of people receiving the favor of God and being able to accomplish something great. Along with all the countless stories of this, the psalms speak much of the necessity of the favor and blessings of God.

> "Let the favor of the Lord our God be upon us,
> and establish the work of our hands upon us; yes,
> establish the work of our hands!" Psalm 90:17

Though this is a psalm of praise, it speaks the deep truth of the favor of God. It is the favor and blessings of God in our lives that establish the work that we do. Without the acceptance and blessings of God, it is impossible to do righteous business. Remember, every minute you have to work, every dollar you have to spend, and every skill you have to use have been bestowed on you by God.

You may do business without seeking the favor of God, but your business will not find the success that God desires your business to have. We can see even in secular business studies that "corporate social responsibility" is valued by most people.[1] The idea that something deeper and more important than mere profit is accepted by even the secular business world should change our perspective on our businesses. How much more should Christians adhere to this understanding? In Mark 10, we can read the story of the rich young ruler. This was a man who was successful by all earthly accounts. He was an excellent example of someone who had done the right things to be successful in his business and life yet was without the greatest blessing of salvation. Jesus made it clear through that story that we may do many things right and yet find ourselves without eternal success. This mindset may often be difficult to have in the heat of battle, as we work furiously to make our businesses successful by any accounts, but with practice and discipline, we can train our minds to frame our businesses in this way.

What is my business accomplishing?

What effect is my business having on me, its stakeholders, and the world?

How can I reframe my perspective to see my business as having an eternal contribution?

Do I see the blessings of God as the foundation for my success, or do I see my own efforts as that foundation?

INTEGRITY: THE KEY TO LASTING SUCCESS

Proverbs 12:3

"No one is established by wickedness,
But the root of the righteous will never be moved."

Righteous business is business with integrity. Anyone who fails to practice integrity will not find true, lasting success. We have mentioned already the fact that our businesses ought to have an eternal impact, but even within the limits of time, we desire our businesses to last as long as possible. This can only happen when we do business with integrity. Integrity refers not only to honesty, but also to the strength of our convictions. That is why this book is called *Righteous Business*, and not just smart business or honest business. That is why this book has the Word of God as its foundation.

Our convictions and morals are the things upon which our honesty rests. Without strong moral convictions, we may be honest only when it pleases or benefits us. However, integrity refers to the habitual practice of honesty and the focus on our morals as we conduct our businesses. This is not something that we can accomplish in the vacuum of our own accountability, however. As we discussed in the previous chapter, it is by the favor of God that our businesses can be successful. Psalm 41:12 says this:

> "But you have upheld me because of my
> integrity, and set me in your presence forever."

This is what we desire as we seek to build a long-lasting business with an eternal impact. To be *set* in the presence of God refers to being stationed and established, to be continually standing in the presence of God. One of the greatest questions regarding integrity in business lies in the definition of morality. If morals are relative, then there is no such thing as integrity. When we understand what the psalmist is saying, we find a means to perfect accountability. By ordering our businesses according to what God's Word says is right, God establishes us in His presence. We are placed *by* God in right-standing *with* God. It is from this position that we can be held accountable as we continue to do business.

There are many examples of a lack of integrity in business practice, and the first example that I think of is Enron.[2] Enron's leaders were guilty of manipulating the numbers of their business in such a way as to make it seem more successful than it was. This was, at first, done in expectation of increasing business success, but quickly became a way of trying to save the business in the face of its astounding lack of success in various business ventures. Integrity is foundational to continuing success, even by the world's limited definition of success. Enron, through its less than honest reporting, was able to find quick success after its establishment, but lost that success just as quickly, with devastating effects on many people.

When we are in the flow of conducting our businesses, we will often find ourselves faced with shortcuts to short-term success. Whether it is presenting or selling something that is not up to standard or falsifying information for any reason, we may find that we are able to do this without any immediate repercussions. Yet, as we see in the Enron example, a lack of integrity is always found out. There are some examples of businesses that appear to be exceptions to this, as they seem to continue finding success in cutting corners. Game developer Bethesda is known for releasing games that are barely finished, fraught with bugs, glitches, and deficient performance. Yet they continue to be a powerhouse in the video game industry. Keep in mind that there is always at least one person holding us accountable to our actions, and that Person is the only One whose opinion and judgement matters.

> "For God will bring every deed into judgement, with
> every secret thing, whether good or evil."
> Ecclesiastes 12:14

Integrity is the key to long-lasting business, and accountability is the key to maintaining integrity. Accountability will be a major part of the discussion in the next chapter, but for now, focus on your morals and standards. Our convictions are the key to our integrity. We may be completely honest and committed to our morals, but if our morals are not based on the source of morality and truth, our integrity is bust. This is why the psalmist speaks of being established in the presence of God. By acknowledging our need for the truth of God's Word and the guidance therein, God helps us by giving us His Word and His Spirit to hold us accountable to good morals and integrity.

On what do I base my moral convictions?

Do I hold myself accountable to an unchanging standard?

Am I committed to long-term success, regardless of the short-term implications?

What steps can I take to ensure that every facet of my business practice is done with integrity?

ASSISTANCE: ALWAYS HAVE A PARTNER

Proverbs 12:4

*"An excellent wife is the crown of her husband,
but she who brings shame is like rottenness in his bones."*

Proverbs 12:4 speaks of the importance of having a godly wife, but whether or not you are married, there is key insight in this verse. Accountability is necessary, as mentioned in the previous chapter. We should always have someone to hold us accountable to doing what is right and to maintaining an excellent work ethic. Especially for the entrepreneur and the manager of a business, accountability is what keeps us from making questionable decisions, even when we do not realize that they are questionable. We always have God holding us accountable to what His Word says is right, but because the repercussions of failing to uphold that standard will not affect us immediately, it is easy to ignore this accountability.

For those who are married, you might feel the need to look for accountability somewhere other than your spouse. We do not want to talk shop when we get home from work. We do not want to discuss the problems of our businesses once we have left the office. For some of you, you may feel as though your spouse lacks the understanding to hold you accountable in your business. They may have no knowledge of how your business operates. However, when you committed to sharing your life with your spouse, you committed to being in business with them. Even if they do not work within your business, they are your businesses partner. At the very least, you chose to marry them because you share a common morality. When it comes to accountability, right is right, regardless of the industry in which your business operates.

If you are not married, it is necessary to find a business partner of some kind. You may not choose to have someone work alongside you in your business, but you need someone with whom you can discuss difficult decisions and obstacles. A person who can serve as a springboard for your ideas, goals, and practices will save you from making many mistakes. For an entrepreneur, this is imperative. This could be someone in the same business, someone you look up to as a diligent worker, or even someone such as the pastor of your church. If you are not an entrepreneur, but are a manager within your business, you will of course have accountability within the management team of your business. I have found that it is also helpful to seek accountability with someone in the same position as you with another company or with another department of your company. This provides accountability that you can trust because of the shared goals, business environment, and standards.

Your friends can also be great accountability partners for your business. They may grow tired of hearing you discuss your business, but if you are honest with them about your desire to have accountability, and if you are wise in limiting how much you talk about your business, your friends can be an excellent source of accountability. Particularly within a friend group, there tends to be an excellent combination of like-mindedness along with diversity of perspective and experience. You may all be friends because of something you have in common, but you each have a unique perspective on life. You will be hard-pressed to find a friend group that does not at least have moral convictions in common. This is the most important aspect of accountability.

Why is it so important that we have this constant accountability? Every one of us must be mindful of the stakeholders in our businesses. Stakeholders are a broader group than shareholders. We owe our shareholders a fiscal responsibility, but we owe our stakeholders so much more. Those who have an interest in the success of our businesses, financial or otherwise, are our stakeholders. This is our family, the community in which our businesses exist and serve, and our God. God is our greatest investor, and it is to Him that we owe success.

Matthew 25:14-30 gives us an understanding of what it means to have a responsibility to our stakeholders. Because the servant in this parable failed to practice excellent business, he failed to produce what he owed his stakeholders. By having accountability partners in place, we have the assistance that we need to keep from making poor business decisions.

Accountability is an important thing, but it does not have to be intimidating. All that is required is the courage to ask someone to help us in making right choices. This is why our spouse ought to be our best accountability partner. Be honest and consistent in communicating with your partner about the challenges and opportunities that you are facing in your business. Even when you do not feel as though you are facing a difficult decision, you may still be facing an impactful decision. Share this with your partner and let them hold you accountable to the results you most want to achieve!

Do I have accountability partners currently?

Do I genuinely want accountability partners in my business?

Have I ever failed to seek accountability in making an impactful decision?

What difference would I see in my business practice if I had consistent accountability?

PERSPECTIVE:
YOUR THOUGHTS
DETERMINE
EVERYTHING

Proverbs 12:5

"The thoughts of the righteous are just;
the counsels of the wicked are deceitful."

Paul McClain, owner of McClain insurance agency, often makes this statement about perspective: "How you view what you do is how you do what you do." In other words, the perspective we have about our businesses determines the way we manage our businesses. We cannot think about our businesses in a negative light and expect to enjoy going to work every day. We cannot think of our businesses as unimportant and yet feel confident about devoting our full effort to our businesses. Paul urges us in Romans 12:2 to transform our minds so that we are able to discern what is good and godly. Studies of leadership and management recognize different frames from which a leader views his organization.[3] Both the Bible and modern business practice recognize the need for a proper mindset about our businesses.

When it comes to our perspectives, most of us do not have substantial changes that need to happen. In my own experience, it is the subconscious feelings that reveal our true perspectives and frames of mind. The things we say and the way we feel when we are stressed, frustrated, or facing significant challenges are the best measure of our perspectives about our businesses. As we do business, it is important that we are aware of this so that we can account for every thought and feeling we have about our businesses. This may seem like an extreme way of thinking, but it is necessary to ensure that we do not find ourselves in a rut of negative thinking. We are blessed to be in business, blessed to be a productive member of society and the world, which means that we must learn to always think in this frame of mind. Whether you are a pessimist or an optimist, learn to be realistic about your perspective. No one ever found themselves more off-track or frustrated with their position than the person who fooled himself into thinking wrongly about his business and his choices.

We are to be optimistic about our businesses. We have been blessed beyond measure and we are building something far bigger than we deserve to be a part of. When we remember that we are undeservingly blessed to be in business and have any amount of success, this changes the way that we think about our businesses, as well as the way we interact with our partners and clients. Proverbs 12:5 tells us that the thoughts and the perspectives of the righteous are just. Jesus echoes this in Matthew 12:35.

> "The good person out of his good treasure
> brings forth good, and the evil person out
> of his evil treasure brings forth evil."

The treasure referred to here by Jesus is representative of our thoughts. When we think good thoughts about our businesses, we will naturally work good things in and through our businesses. This is spoken of by Jesus as a basic principle for the way our mind and actions correlate to each other. We spoke of accountability before, and Jesus here goes on to say that we will be held accountable for the negativity of mind that leads to negative and destructive words.

If you are like me, you may struggle with changing your mindset, frame of reference, or perspective. It is obvious why positivity is better than negativity, but this is such a difficult change to make. Looking to scriptures for direction and encouragement has been the greatest help for me, and will be for you, as well. First, we must recognize that changing our perspective is not merely a matter of changing some of the thoughts we often have. In order to profoundly change our mindset, we must change the source of those thoughts. Ephesians 4:23 tells us that the spirit of our mind must be renewed. This refers to the same total transformation that Paul wrote about in Romans 12:2 but highlights the spiritual nature of the process. Our mind is something other than physical, so we must change it with something other than physical.

What is other than physical that we can allow or apply to change our perspective? Colossians 3:2 tells us to fix our minds on things above, not on earthly things. We are again reminded of the supremacy and necessity of God in the ability to conduct righteous business. There is no mindset or perspective that is eternally effective other than the mind of the Eternal One. When we allow our mindset to be determined by earthly things or other people, we are limiting our perspective to what can be understood by earthly things. When we allow our mindset to be determined by God, the Word of God and the Will of God, we can have an unchanging foundation for a righteous, positive mindset.

This mindset is not one that immediately comes with receiving salvation or committing ourselves to do righteous business. A good and godly perspective takes practice, practice, practice. This is why we ought to allow the Word of God and the Body of Christ to help hold us accountable, as we discussed in the previous chapter. By placing ourselves in a place of godly perspective, our perspective will follow suit.

Does my perspective consist of a godly mix of positivism and realism?

Is my perspective easily swayed by circumstances?

What or who do I allow to alter my mindset?

How do I view what I do?

SPEAK WISELY:
WHAT YOU SAY
OR DON'T SAY

Proverbs 12:6

"The words of the wicked lie in wait for blood,
but the mouth of the upright delivers them."

Proverbs 12:6 speaks of the words of the wicked as a trap placed specifically to harm or demean someone else. Often in the heat of a workday, it can be easy to make your own project or team look good by simply tearing down another team or team member. When I consider this kind of behavior, I feel as though I am above acting this low. You may feel the same way. You would never make it a habit to tear others down simply to make yourself look better. However, if we really examine the things we say about our coworkers, employees, or peers, we will find that we speak negatively about others more often than we realize.

An example of this can be seen during a meeting of managers. One manager knows they are struggling with keeping their own team up to standard. Their contribution to the meeting is to emphasize any issues they see with another manager's team. This kind of speech may be framed in such a way as to seem helpful to the other manager, yet it is really an attempt to bring down the positive results of one person to minimize our own negative results. Speaking in this way towards other people is all too common in our day-to-day interaction with our peers, yet it is so detrimental to positive organizational development.

If we make it a habit to speak this way about others, it reveals other issues that we have deep in our heart. Issues such as pride, fear of conflict, or insecurity can cause us to put on a front in the way that we speak. These are topics that will be discussed in other chapters, but here I would like to examine the things that are not being said that ought to be said. The words of the wicked lie as a trap, but Proverbs says that the speech of the righteous delivers them. As a struggling young manager, I hated reporting my team's shortcomings to any other manager, regardless of their level within the organization. Rather than be honest about the struggles that were causing us to be substandard, I would point to the shortcomings of others. I was saying one thing so that I could avoid saying another thing. This kept me from getting the support that I needed. This kept me from getting the coaching and resources that my team needed.

For a leader or manager, there will always be things that you do not want to say because of what it reveals about the success of your team or your leadership. Especially for an entrepreneur, the honest truth about the state of your business might make you look foolish, unskilled, or lazy. Yet it is when we are able to say those things that most need to be said that we are able to be rescued by our own words. When we are willing to speak freely about our needs, we give others the opportunity to help us. James wrote that we do not have because we do not ask, and I believe that principle can apply to our business interactions. We will never have the appropriate resources, support, and training if we consistently fail to communicate those needs and opportunities with our teams.

As important as it is to recognize what needs to be said, and then to say it, we sometimes must first learn the skill of saying nothing at all. It can be difficult to say the right things if our habit is to blurt out the wrong things. Proverbs 12:6 speaks of the words of the righteous, but I would suggest that for those who particularly struggle with having negative words, saying nothing is the logical first step in changing our speech towards righteousness. I have sat through many meetings without saying a single word not because I felt like not participating, but because I wanted to tear others down to make myself look better.

You may have already come to this realization about your speech, but I would encourage you to take inventory of your verbal interactions today. You may find that you still speak negatively about others in extreme stress or struggles. We read in James 3:2 that no man is perfect in his speaking, which means that each of us must be reminded to watch our mouths. Our speech has great power to build up others, as well as ourselves. In the same way, it can tear down so easily. If you do struggle with speaking negatively about others, especially when you are struggling, start changing your habits of speech by saying nothing at all. Consider what most needs to be said, what is most helpful to the organization and to your team and say only that. Having learned to refrain from speaking negatively, be courageous enough to say what is difficult to say: your team needs help, is facing an obstacle, or is not performing to standards. This is a challenging thing to admit, but it is what you, your team, and your organization needs to hear the most.

When was the last time I pointed out someone else's shortcomings?

When was the last time I was honest about my own shortcomings?

Has there ever been a time that I asked for help and saw my business succeed as a result?

What struggles am I facing now that I have not been honest about revealing or confronting?

LONGEVITY: LONG-TERM FOCUS

Proverbs 12:7

*"The wicked are overthrown and are no more,
but the house of the righteous will stand."*

We have covered the importance of having integrity and understand that a lack of integrity will not bring enduring success; Proverbs 12:7 echoes that concept. Some businesses that are not conducted in righteousness crumble because of intentionally deceitful practices, but there are some that are easily defeated by adversity, even if they are not intentionally wicked. Every business will face adversity and challenges, but Proverbs here tells us that it is the righteous who will have longevity in their business. A well-known parable helps us highlight the difference between a business that will endure and a business that will not.

> "Everyone then who hears these words of mine
> and does them will be like a wise man who built
> his house on the rock. And the rain fell, and
> the floods came, and the winds blew and beat
> on that house, but it did not fall, because it had
> been founded on the rock." Matthew 7:24-25

Jesus made it clear that the foundation upon which we build our businesses makes the difference in the longevity of that business. He even goes on to say in the next few verses that simply failing to lay down a righteous foundation will cause a house, or business, to crumble in any storm. Intentionality in the foundation of our businesses roots us in something that is unchanging and immovable. We often perceive wicked practice as an intentional lack of righteousness, but failing to adhere to biblical principles, even in ignorance, is failing to build on a firm foundation.

The foundation of our businesses refers not just to the things we did in establishing the business, or the early days. The foundation of our businesses, especially in the context of this parable, refers to the foundation upon which we lay each brick. Every decision we make, every value we uphold, and every motive we have reflects the foundation upon which we are building. It is interesting that even in secular business culture, many businesses are changing their focus from pure profit to a more complex goal of "creating value." However, a business defines value, this is the modern way to measure success. We will discuss this in depth two chapters from now.

It can be difficult to know what decisions to make in order to keep your businesses rooted on the rock, and we may find ourselves struggling to feel as though we are even capable of making the correct decisions. If you recognize this feeling, you are just like every other leader and manager. Thankfully, we have a Rock to which we can look for an unwavering reference as we navigate our businesses through an ever-changing sociocultural landscape. Jesus uses specific language and imagery here as He tells this parable, language that resembles Proverbs 10:25, 30 and 11:21. The Word of God, written and living, gives us a foundation from which to build a successful, long-lasting business. This book hopefully serves as an excellent example for the wisdom available in scriptures for leaders and managers. We have referenced Romans 12:2 already in this book, but it is worth revisiting. When we need good discernment on what decisions to make, the Word of God not only gives us insight, but it also conditions our mind to grow in its ability to make good decisions. In other words, as we continue to study the scriptures and apply them to our lives and business, we get better at understanding how to apply the Word to our lives and business. The law of diminishing returns does not apply to the wisdom of the Word of God.

Longevity requires consistency. This is a challenge and an encouragement as we build our businesses on a firm foundation. It is a challenge because it means that we must continue to make careful, often difficult, decisions. To continue making decisions that go against the culture of the business world around us can cause us to doubt ourselves, feel handicapped, or seem foolish to the world. Yet we understand that the truth of scripture guarantees the longevity of our businesses when we conduct it with a righteous foundation. This is an encouragement to us because it means that when we make a mistake, it is only a small part of our whole story. When we fail to discern the right decision, we have not ruined our businesses. If our businesses are built on the rock, it will take more than our own ignorance, doubt, and shortcomings to be destroyed. Being rooted on the foundation of biblical wisdom ensures that we are established in the presence of God. By focusing on the long-term goals and motives of our businesses, we are able to create a business with longevity. When our foundation is righteous, we can impact eternity.

Are my goals and motives eternally focused?

Do my business decisions reflect that I am building on the foundation of the Word of God?

Have I ever felt short-term hindrances because I made long-term decisions?

What decision can I make today that will increase the longevity of my business?

COMMENDATION: GOOD BUSINESS PRACTICE AND RECOGNITION

Proverbs 12:8

*"A man is commended according to his good sense,
but one of twisted mind is despised."*

Especially in the age of social media and instant information, recognition and fame, no matter how shallow or short-lived, can be easy to come by. Sites like SoundCloud can give an amateur musician the ability to release their own song and see it go viral. YouTube provides a place for creatives to establish a platform from which they can become well-known or loved in their field. Our natural desire is to be well-liked, praised, or otherwise commended. Today's verse tells us that those who practice good sense will receive commendation from their peers. The phrase *good sense* refers to wise judgement, expertise, and everything that is good business practice. To receive commendation from the world can be a dangerous thing, as evidenced by the troubled lives of so many celebrities. However, we cannot deny the truth of this verse: that good business sense draws commendation.

As we begin to receive commendation from our peers, our motives will be challenged. We will be tempted with pride and tempted to work towards a separate set of goals and standards than we ought. Though it may not be apparent right away, this can bring our businesses down from the success that earned us the commendation of our peers in the first place. We must avoid this at all costs, but how are we to manage this commendation if the Bible says that it is well-deserved? Colossians 3:23-24 reminds us of the motivations we should have, as well as the source of our greatest commendation.

> "Whatever you do, work heartily, as for the
> Lord and not for men, knowing that from the
> Lord you will receive the inheritance as your
> reward. You are serving the Lord Christ."

If the primary motivation for our good business practice is to achieve worldly goals or material success, the commendation of men will be the greatest reward we will ever receive. Colossians warns against this by reminding us that we do not work for men, nor do we work with the Lord as merely an advisor. We do our work for the express purpose of pleasing and honoring God, as well as advancing His plan for Creation. We have mentioned this before, but even if your businesses are something as simple as retail or general labor, you are providing a product or service that enables people to carry out what God has called them to do. Every job that God has appointed humankind to work is important in His Kingdom. With this understanding, we have no excuse. We ought to do our work for His sake, and nothing else.

One of the simplest ways to maintain the right motives as we receive commendation for our good business is to stay in the Word. The more we study the Word and Will of God, the easier it will be to keep that as our main focus and motivation. Even the simple reminder of Colossians 3:23 is a prompt to refocus our attention on what really matters as we go into a new workday. As we have continued to discuss throughout this study, keeping our focus on Christ as we seek to do good business will turn into righteous leaders and turn our businesses into ones with eternal impact.

As we work to keep our focus on Christ and not on the commendation of our peers, we should not neglect to use the recognition we are earning as effectively as possible. Worldly commendation should not be what shapes us but should be a marker of how we are shaping the world. The fact that people are recognizing excellence in our leadership and business means that we are influencing our peers and our industry. God has given us this ability as another crucial way that we can serve and honor Him. Not only by giving Him the glory for our successes, but also by furthering the effect of righteous business in the world. Grow your righteous business to make a righteous change in your industry, your community, your family, and your country. Grow your righteous business to generate more righteous leaders who will have the same effect in their own circles. This is a surefire way to see your business explode in biblically grounded success. Long-term success is part of the inheritance from the Lord that Colossians speaks of.

Ephesians 6:8 reminds us, in the same theme as Colossians, that whatever good anyone does, he will receive back from the Lord. This is a great encouragement as we fight to have excellent business with right motives. As we inevitably gain recognition from the world, we can trust that we will be tremendously blessed by the Lord when we continue to work solely for His sake, and not for the world. Commendation is not a terrible thing, but pride is. Short-sighted business, which naturally results from a focus on the short-lived fame of the world, is the result of failing to abide by what Proverbs 12, Colossians 3, and Ephesians 6 all teach.

Have I ever received commendation for my work?

How did that commendation change the way I thought about myself and my business?

How did that commendation change my business goals and standards?

Am I using my worldly recognition to glorify God through my leadership and business?

HONESTY: DEFINE YOUR SUCCESS

Proverbs 12:9

*"Better to be lowly and have a servant
than to play the great man and lack bread."*

In this chapter we will discuss honesty, examining the importance of being honest with ourselves. I have known many people who were willing to work extremely hard, but not willing to honestly assess the progress of their business towards its goals. When we hustle without focus, we find ourselves with no real growth in our businesses. We may feel as though we have accomplished remarkable things, but our businesses do not reflect this. Just as important as arduous work is close scrutiny of our results. Managers and leaders need to measure their results against their goals and standards on a very regular basis, or else risk becoming stagnant, or even wayward. If we fail to do this, we are running our businesses on autopilot, allowing circumstances and outside influences to determine the trajectory of our businesses.

Leaders who find themselves in this situation are often reactive, rather than proactive. Being a proactive leader means working with our eyes up, understanding what is happening in our businesses and our industry. This requires honesty with ourselves about our progress. Are we growing, adapting, and changing in a way that matches what is happening in the world around us? Or are we allowing ourselves to feel a false sense of fulfillment based only on the level of effort we are giving? We discussed success in the previous chapter and understand the importance of a proper focus and right motives as we do business. However, defining our success is crucial. Doing the wrong things with the right intentions is just as hurtful as doing the right things for the wrong reason. It is important then not only to have the right motives, but also the right goals.

Jesus says in Matthew 6:19-21 that our goal should be to accumulate treasures in Heaven, not on earth. Of course, this does not mean that we are not to do business well enough to make a profit while we are here on earth. It does mean that we are to work for the goal of gaining wealth greater than only what can be found in the world. This echoes what was mentioned previously about the emerging focus on corporate social responsibility. With this in mind, we must ask ourselves how we define the success of our businesses. You may point to your key performance indicators and say that reaching them is success, but I would challenge you to look deeper. What defines your key performance indicators? How do you define key performance? What makes those numbers more important than any other numbers?

> "I press on toward the goal for the prize of the
> upward call of God in Christ Jesus."
> Philippians 3:14

It is important that we build habits that facilitate consistency in being honest with ourselves about our goals and progress. Regularly take time to review your goals and compare them with your metrics. Just as a business owner must continue to revisit their original business plan, so should every manager revisit their goals. You may feel as though you are doing well enough in reaching your goals because your business has not failed yet, but how much better could you be doing? When Paul said that he pressed on toward his goal, he said that he did it in such a way as to honor God's high standards for us. Was Paul perfect? No. Read the rest of Philippians 3. But Paul understood that the circumstances of life will force us to reevaluate our goals, challenge our standards, and adjust our plans.

Another great practice is to share your goals with every member of your team. In fact, if your team does not have a clear understanding of your goals and the reason for those goals, you are short-changing yourself as a leader and manager. You may understand your goals well enough to drive your team towards those goals, but if you fail to share that vision with your team, you are leading a blind team, no matter how talented they are as individuals. By sharing your goals with your team, you can gain greater insight into where your business stands in making progress towards those goals. The perspectives of your team members will help shape the way you lead and develop the business in an ever-changing world.

One common hindrance that leaders face in forcing themselves to regularly review their goals and progress is that they are afraid to see the negative results. Just as being honest with others about our team's standing enables others to support us, so also does being honest with ourselves about our team enable us to grow our team. Whether your team or business is large or small, you have a lot of information to review on a regular basis. This may seem tedious, but if you care about the long-term success of your business, you will learn to find fulfillment in poring over your metrics. I have even found that reviewing my team's performance metrics gave me insight into their personal lives as well.

One team member who always performed superbly had a significant dip in performance as I reviewed metrics one week. When I mentioned this with them, they revealed personal struggles that they had been having with their living situation. By being honest with myself about my business I was able to address an issue that affected my business, as well as provide support to a valued team member who was in a tough situation. This is just one example of the incredible insight that we gain when we work with our eyes up, being honest with ourselves about the standing of our businesses.

Some leaders may struggle with this simply because they struggle with understanding some of the numbers of their business. That is okay. No one understands everything about their field. We only fail when we fail to learn. This is something I have to remind myself of constantly. Find someone who can help you review your business growth regularly, and you will soon find that you have learned more about your business than you would on your own. The most important thing is being honest with yourself. This will set you up for success and growth beyond what you ever expected.

What are my goals for my business? Why?

Am I on track to meet those goals?

When was the last time I defined and reviewed my key performance indicators?

Am I willing to be honest with myself about my progress and failures as I develop myself and my business?

RESPECT: APPRECIATING YOUR BUSINESS

Proverbs 12:10

"Whoever is righteous has regard for the life of his beast, but the mercy of the wicked is cruel."

Every business has resources and assets that enable it to function, grow, and find success. No matter what product or service your businesses provides, you have certain inputs that allow those outputs. Proverbs defines what may be an often-overlooked aspect of righteous business: respect for our assets and resources. The context for this verse lies in the type of economy in which the original audience would have operated. The ancient Israelites were an agrarian people, and the tools of their trade looked vastly different than the tools of most businesspeople in modern times. Rather than assets such as office equipment, company vehicles, and factories, the Israelites would have had rudimentary tools and pack animals to help operate those tools. In both cases, the wisdom of Proverbs 12:10 is incredibly important to understand and apply.

Having regard for one's animals, in ancient times, would have meant caring for those animals with the understanding that those animals were the key to being successful in whatever business an Israelite would have found themselves. The Israelites understood that these animals were blessings from God, and they knew the importance of stewarding those blessings well. Feeding and sheltering the animals were just as important as understanding how best to utilize the labor provided by the pack animals. This ancient context gives us a simple view of two key aspects of respecting our resources. Not only do we ensure the upkeep or well-being of our assets, but we also work for the development of our assets. Whether tools of the trade or employees, we ought to be good stewards of those things that enable us to do business.

In modern business, this concept may be a little more difficult to apply readily. Rather than caring for animals, we are tasked with caring for assets such as equipment, investments, or buildings. This will require more of a business understanding than just caring for animals, but that is natural considering the increase in complexity from an agrarian business to one such as that with which we are most familiar. Our devotion to understanding our businesses should give us a deeper appreciation for our tools and resources, as well as enable us to know how to steward them well. From simply keeping tools and equipment in good working order to planning carefully how to maximize output by properly utilizing our assets, we steward our resources with a reverence fitting them as blessings from God.

The fact that our resources are blessings from God should change the perspective we have of them. Rather than see our resources as expendable or ordinary, we see them as a great gift, enabling us to be successful. All of our assets are part of God's creation, and we are called to steward the assets as well as the creation. By doing business with this mindset of respect and appreciation, we are able to grow our businesses, develop our assets, and participate in the redemption of the world. We see this entire process best summed up in the way we steward our greatest asset: our employees and team members. By respecting and developing our team members, we are at once both stewarding our assets as well as redeeming creation. Our employees are members of our team and members of our society, and we owe it to them to be the best stewards we can be. When we became leaders, we assumed that great Christian responsibility of properly stewarding everything placed under our care.

The phrase *has regard* in this verse carries a very intimate notion. Throughout the Old Testament, it is used in numerous ways, but always referring to a deep understanding of someone or something. This goes back to the previously mentioned idea of understanding the most effective ways to utilize our equipment, and investments. However, it applies especially to the stewarding of our employees. We cannot truly steward them if we do not make a conscious effort to know them well. Every one of our employees, even if they are performing the same job function for our businesses, has different goals and ambitions. They also have different skill sets and perspectives on life and on the business. By knowing them well, we can tailor our leadership most effectively towards developing them to be the best that they were created to be.

This concept can be exceedingly difficult to put into practice, no matter how we feel about it in our minds. We may feel very strongly that this is the best way to lead and manage, but in the heat of a hectic business day, our focus turns quickly to metrics and other business factors. At the end of the day, we will quickly find overlooked, struggling employees who wish they had some support, whether in a work matter or a personal matter. We owe it to God and to our employees to steward them, care for them, and develop them. Everything we need to do business has been given to us by God, and we have the supreme responsibility of honoring His blessing with excellent stewardship. This requires first that we have a deep respect and appreciation for what we have at hand.

Do I appreciate my assets as the blessings they are?

How can I steward the tools of my business better?

Am I providing an atmosphere of care for my team members?

Am I developing my abilities in stewarding my assets?

VISION: CLEAR VISION AND CONSISTENT EFFORT

Proverbs 12:11

*"Whoever works his land will have plenty of bread,
but he who follows worthless pursuits lacks sense."*

P roverbs 12:11 speaks of the righteousness and success of the man who works his land. Working land, of course, is doing our work. For the Israelites, an agrarian society, working one's land was conducting one's business. If you can picture the farmer working his land, you will see demanding work, consistent work, and purposeful work. These are the things that we must learn, even in our modernized societies, if we are to be successful in business. To do these things well requires more than simply hard work, however. If all you want to be concerned with is working hard, do not be a leader. Be someone else's employee.

As a leader, we have a lot of work to do, and it is challenging work. But we also have the responsibility of deciding how to focus our efforts, which goes hand-in-hand with the previous chapter's discussion on stewardship. We must have a clear vision of not only our goals, but also the means by which we will achieve those goals. We have already discussed the importance of understanding the best goals for maintaining longevity in our businesses, and we will now zoom in to learn how to discern the right actions necessary for reaching those goals.

The importance of clear vision, encompassing the ends as well as the means, is to avoid wasting time on unnecessary projects and actions. This is what Proverbs 12:11 warns about. Many leaders, if they are not careful to discern, cast, and maintain a clear vision, will waste time, either themselves or through the work of their team members, on actions that do not help the organization reach its desired end goals. The trouble with this notion is that we often struggle with deciding which actions to take. How can we know if they will not be successful in contributing to our desired end goals? One way is by understanding the industry in which you operate and learning from the mistakes of others, but this can only help to a certain extent. Every organization is different, and we will have different means of achieving our similar goals.

"The heart of man plans his way,
but the Lord establishes his steps."
Proverbs 16:9

We are expected to make discernments about how we should act, how we should conduct our businesses, and what means we should take to reach our desired goals. However, God does not expect us to do this solely in our own knowledge. In fact, the Bible instructs us not to rely on our own understanding. Rather, we are to learn how to discern what the will of God is by applying ourselves to His Word regularly and seeking Him out in prayer constantly. As we consider what plans to make, we do so with the help of God and His Spirit. We will inevitably be wrong in our discerning, at times, but this is how we learn how to be better leaders. As we habitually seek God's will for ourselves and our businesses, we will become better leaders and better businesspeople.

When we find that we have discerned incorrectly, we do not need to feel frustrated or less-than. Eric Mason, founder of Epiphany Fellowship, says that part of this process is learning to be okay with being wrong.[4] None of us would intentionally make poor decisions for our businesses, yet none of us are perfect. Certain things may seem important or relevant as we make decisions, and we will not find out that we are wrong until after we have made them. Even when we make decisions that are objectively good, they may not necessarily be a part of the plan that God desires for us. This is when we must learn to accept that we are not the top of our businesses' organizational chart. No matter your position in your business, God is sovereign, and He is our ultimate shareholder.

The idea of continuing to practice good discernment has already been brought up, but this highlights another crucial aspect of success in our businesses. Once we have begun the cyclical process of casting vision, we must be consistent in our efforts to maintain and reach that vision. Part of working land means that the land must be plowed, planted, watered, harvested, then plowed again. The process is a never-ending cycle of upkeep and maintenance. Discipline cannot happen without consistency, vision cannot happen without consistency, success cannot happen without consistency; consistency is key. There are so many things we learn to do as we develop our businesses and leadership but doing those things once each will never lead us to success. Even casting vision must be done consistently if we are to succeed. Craig Groeschel, of Life Church, says this:

"Successful people do consistently what normal people do occasionally."

There is no better way to end a discussion on vision and consistency than with this quote, understanding it, and applying it.

Do I have a clear vision for what I need to achieve and how I need to achieve it?

Are there any actions or projects on which I am wasting resources?

Do I regularly allow God to shape my vision for myself and my business?

Am I consistently defining and pursuing the vision for my business?

CONTENTMENT: FOCUS ON YOUR OWN RESULTS

Proverbs 12:12

*"Whoever is wicked covets the spoil of evildoers,
but the root of the righteous bears fruit."*

A s we work to increase our success and grow our businesses, we cannot neglect the discipline of contentment. A healthy balance exists between desiring to see our businesses grow and appreciating what we already have. The key to this is remembering the eternal goal that undergirds all of our other goals. Our work is for the Lord, and it is His business that we are about. It is because of this that we are able to both develop a successful business and be content with what we have.

To desire something other than what you have earned or been given is to covet. We understand that coveting is sinful, yet we are programmed to covet as a way of setting goals and shaping ambitions. The American Dream can very quickly become a mindset of covetousness if we are not careful to keep our focus where it ought to be. Proverbs 12:12 uses two important words to differentiate between the ways that we can see our businesses grow. The unrighteous person covets the spoil of others. Spoils are things that are taken, not earned, and this is how an unrighteous business may find short-term success. Any material gains that are taken and not earned will only be temporary. This is not how we are to grow our businesses.

None of us would desire to steal from other businesses or leaders in order to increase our material wealth, but I would argue that we often do steal without realizing it. Though we may not steal their cash or products, it can be amazingly easy to steal an idea or steal credit from another organization. For a businessperson who is always keeping up with what is happening within his industry, stealing ideas may happen passively, without regard to who owns those ideas. Though it is wise to learn from others and adapt to changes in our environment, we need to ensure that we are not unfairly taking gains from someone else's efforts.

In speaking of the righteous person, this verse says that the root of the righteous will bear fruit. This is where we find a balance between growth and contentment. Proverbs 12 has already spoken of the necessity of working your own land, and the same language is used here. When a person works to invest in their business, they are planting seeds that will grow over time, so long as they are careful to cultivate that investment. We may look around and see that other businesses are finding greater success or earning higher profits, but that does not give us an excuse to cease cultivating the seeds that we have planted in our own business. Regardless of how much fruit you see right now, you can be content with your results because you know that the seeds you planted will bear fruit.

Patience is necessary when planting anything, as no two businesses will produce exactly the same fruit at the same time. Our contentment is not in the fruit itself, but in the root. If you have established your business with righteous intentions and practices, and your goals are godly, then you have already begun to produce and benefit from the eternal fruit produced by righteous business. Even if all we can see is tilled dirt, we can see successful progress.

> "But godliness with contentment is great gain,
> for we brought nothing into the world,
> and we cannot take anything out of the world."
> 1 Timothy 6:6-7

What fruit have we reaped if all we can see is tilled ground? How can we be content without yet receiving material gain? By practicing righteousness in our businesses, we are at once making an eternal investment and receiving an eternal reward. We are storing up for ourselves treasures in Heaven as we learn to be godly and content with our businesses and leadership. Though material gains can be important while we are here on earth, they are not the most important value that we work to create. The book of 1 Timothy goes on to explain that love of money is a root of evil. Money and worldly wealth are not inherently evil, but our desire for those things is evil when they override our desire for heavenly riches. Material value is not the highest value we work to produce.

The value with which we are to be most concerned and most content is eternal. A thriving righteous business produces both material value, in the form of profits and other capital gains, as well as eternal value. This eternal value is much harder to interpret at times, but it is easiest to see in the effects it has on us and on our stakeholders. Are we giving our employees a reasonable income and improving their quality of life? Are we growing as godly leaders and taking care of our family? Are we improving the conditions of our community by positively contributing to a healthy local economy? These are the things in which we can find contentment, even without regard to our profits. By learning to focus on all of our results, not just the obvious profits, we can find immense contentment in our righteous business.

Am I focused on my own results, or do I compare my success against the success of others?

Do I measure my success by material gains or by eternal investments?

In what ways do I steal from others to increase my success?

Am I content with the success and growth of my business?

SPEAK YOUR HEART: SPEECH REVEALS CHARACTER

Proverbs 12:13

*"An evil man is ensnared by the transgression of his lips,
but the righteous escapes from trouble."*

For leaders, words carry great weight. We are not only responsible for doing a job; we are responsible for those who are responsible for doing the job.[5] If we are not careful about how we speak to and about others, as well as our businesses, we will find ourselves trying to climb out of a great many holes we have dug. The power of our speech as leaders lies in the fact that we cast and communicate the vision of our organization, we train and discipline team members, and we edify individuals as we interact with them. With these great responsibilities, our character matters more than it ever would if we were not leaders.

Though none of us are perfect, we must strive to be in our manner of speech. We all will stumble and allow ourselves to speak negatively, but how we speak consistently defines our character. Team members will forgive us for occasional mistakes if they understand that our heart is not in those occasions. We may say positive things often, but if we habitually say negative things more often than we speak positively, our businesses will suffer. Our team members will not trust the positive things that we say, and our words will begin to lose power. Not only will we find that we are unable to encourage, but our words will draw less respect. Positive speech will become hypocrisy if we allow ourselves to live with a habitually negative attitude.

> "With it we bless our Lord and Father, and
> with it we curse people who are made in the
> likeness of God. From the same mouth come
> blessing and cursing. My brothers, these
> things ought not to be so." James 3:9-10

In a chapter dealing with the power of our speech, James 3 points out the hypocrisy that we experience often and display more often. It is much easier to spot this behavior in someone else because we listen to understand when someone speaks to us. However, we say only what we believe we understand and agree with. (Unless we make it a habit to intentionally be hypocritical.) As we interact with our team members, talk about our businesses, and cast vision for our organization, we cannot be effective if we allow negative and positive speech to pour out. Negative speech will ensnare us, disabling our ability to lead.

James 3 goes on to say in verse thirteen that our words and our actions correlate to and display our wisdom. Even a new leader can gain ground in earning respect and love from followers by the way that they speak. When I was a Digital Operations Manager in retail, there was a time that I knew little about Digital Operations. My team, seasoned in that environment, understood the operations better than I did. What I had in my toolbelt was leadership and management education and experience. That education and experience, coupled with a habit of speaking well about my team and my organization, gave me a place from which to lead my team effectively as I learned the details of my new leadership environment. Rather than see me as someone who did not know as much as them, my team saw me as someone who could help them if they were patient in helping me. My speech saved me from an otherwise difficult experience with a new team.

There are three specific ways in which we reveal our character through our speech. By being aware of those areas and understanding the power of our speech, I hope to help you begin to change your habits of speaking. This will at once both shape your character and improve your ability to reveal it effectively. First, we reveal our character in conversation with our peers and team members. The way we casually speak about other team members and the organization, as a whole, reveals how we really feel about things. This also applies to the way we speak about our customers or clients. If your business involves customer service, you have an immense potential for diminishing your character or strengthening it in the way that you speak about those customers. We may be the most encouraging person in the world for our team and we may love our businesses, but when we speak ill of customers, we reveal a heart that does not genuinely love all people and care about their needs.

Second, we reveal our character when we allow negative conversation among team members. Though we may not participate in those conversations, our allowance of them reveals a tolerance for something that is not acceptable. We cannot control our team members, and we certainly cannot create good character in them, but we can be an example of good character for them to emulate. After all, we are their leader! Stop allowing your team members to habitually speak poorly of each other, the organization, or customers. Instead, ensure that they see you as being approachable. When they feel that they can approach you with concerns or frustrations, they will be able to find resolutions for the problems that they are experiencing.

Last, we reveal our character when we fail to contribute positively in our manner of speaking. This echoes what was discussed about Proverbs 12:6, but it bears repeating. It is important for us, as leaders, to go out of our way to say positive things about our team, our businesses, and our customers. We recognize and share positivity, we remind team members of how our organization creates value for everyone, and we edify at every opportunity. It is impossible to say that we have a habit of speaking positively if we actually have a habit of not speaking at all. This is a personal struggle that I am working to overcome. It is easy to be quiet, but positive thoughts are more than multiplied when we share them with others. Let your righteous character overflow from your heart and out of your mouth as you interact with your team.

Our speech holds greater power than we realize. We hold power to shape our businesses, as well as our team members and the community we serve. Begin practicing habits of positive speech today as you interact with your team and see the change in their attitude towards you and your business.

What positive verbal contributions have I made to my business lately?

Do I have habits of speech that reveal a lack of character, integrity, or commitment to my business?

Do I allow others on my team to build these kinds of negative habits?

How can I reveal righteous character in the way that I speak to my team about my business today?

FULFILLMENT: FIND FULFILLMENT IN THE FRUITS OF YOUR WORK

Proverbs 12:14

*"From the fruit of his mouth a man is satisfied with good,
and the work of a man's hand comes back to him."*

A s we learn and strive to work righteously, we must learn to find fulfillment in our work, trusting that we will experience results. The typical business culture equates success with value creation, and the primary value of concern is profit. Though many businesses are growing to value much more than numerical growth, end of quarter and end of year figures are the major fulcrums on which we pivot. Until we reach the end and can see the final results, we struggle to experience real satisfaction or fulfillment. A good day cannot rescue a bad week. Yet, this is not how scripture encourages us to view our work.

Proverbs 12:14 tells us that the work of our hands comes back to us. This is true for all people, no matter what. You reap what you sow. What we plant will grow into something, but it is up to our efforts to determine if we will produce good or bad fruit. This is a promise given to us by God. When we understand this promise, our perspective on our work should change. Regardless of your industry, there is a wait between your sowing and your reaping. There is a process that you must follow in order to experience results. Even in your paycheck, you must sow, wait, then reap the direct deposit. This is inherent in any kind of work, even spiritually. We receive salvation, but are not immediately perfect, sinless, and transported up to Heaven. We must endure a process, sowing with the understanding that we will one day reap. This is one reason it is so important to always be increasing in excellence in our field of work. The better we understand the specific processes of our industry and business, the easier it will be to plant and cultivate for a good harvest.

Once we have planted, we must wait. But we must also trust. There are two aspects to trust when it comes to our businesses. If we are really experts in our field, we can trust our business acumen, as well as the history of our industry. If your business is one that has a history of being successful, you can sow into that business with trust in the fact that it will pay off. We can invest confidently in a business model that is sure. We should not neglect this aspect of trust in our businesses. It can be so easy to use our trust in God as an excuse for poor research and unwise investments. God has given us the resources to plant, but He does not desire us to plant without due diligence.

A friend of mine started a tech repair business and was able to find success fairly quickly. He hired someone to run the business, since he was already employed full-time elsewhere, and the new manager was able to help this new business owner earn back his investment within the first couple of years. In business, that is a short time to reach self-sufficiency. In personal finances, that is a long time to be without all of that investment money. However, my friend was not panicked. He was confident because he had prayed about the decision and investment. But he was able to be even more confident because he researched the industry. He was prepared to sow into something and then wait. And he is now reaping the benefits of that trust in the process.

> "Tell the righteous that it shall be well with them,
> for they shall eat the fruit of their deeds."
> Isaiah 3:10

Trusting in God must go hand-in-hand with trusting our business knowledge. Though business acumen requires keen analytical skills and strategic thinking, we are working for something greater than earthly success. If we are truly doing righteous business, we are careful to invest only in those things that are in accordance with God's plan for us and for those within our organization. We can look back on the times that God has blessed us. We can look back on the times that God has blessed others. This increases our trust in God, as well as in the process in which He has led us to take part.

Knowing that we will reap a harvest from what we have sown can increase our trust in the process and help us to find satisfaction in what we are doing. However, I would encourage you to seek for a deeper fulfillment in the work that you are doing. If you know that you are striving to do business according to righteous principles, you are already reaping a reward. If you are careful to abide by godly principles in your business practice, you are creating value for yourself, for others, and for the Kingdom of God, even before what you planted is ready for harvest. As Isaiah 3 says, we are promised that we will reap a reward, but that whole chapter is about judgement from the Lord. Isaiah is pronouncing a judgement on those who are living in an unrighteous way yet throws in the fact that the righteous are being looked on by God with favor. Not because of their fruits, but because of their motives. Because they are striving for righteousness, they are in a different category. They are in favor with God and are promised an abundance.

We are fulfilled by the results of our work, but also by the way we do our work. As we continue to work righteously, we will get better and better at working righteously. We learn to manage our time differently, have a changed perspective on our direction and investments, and value our people differently. The act of participating in the process increases our ability to be productive in that process. The more we invest wisely, the more we will have available to invest. As I am careful to write each chapter of this book, I can trust that when I sit down to write the next chapter, I will be an even better author than when I wrote this chapter. As much as I look forward to finding satisfaction in the completion and publishing of this book, I can find so much joy and fulfillment in the process of writing it. Why? I am an author who is practicing his ability to write, increasing my capacity for writing better content. While the publishing of this book will certainly be an exciting achievement, the act of writing it is the longer-lasting investment for the skills with which I have been blessed.

We should be satisfied with our results. We were diligent, the process worked, God was faithful, and we have provision. It is a wonderful thing to reap a good harvest from what you have sown. But do not neglect to appreciate the process as you participate. We have much to learn about our businesses, and there is much satisfaction to be found in learning to do our business better. Find fulfillment in the work that you do, not because of the results, but because of the investment.

Do I find more contentment in the results than I do in the process?

Is the extent of my satisfaction in my work based on the extent of my results?

Do I trust that righteous business will produce the best results?

COUNSEL:
SEEK EXPERT
ADVICE

Proverbs 12:15

*"The way of a fool is right in his own eyes,
but a wise man listens to advice."*

Today's verse describes differences between the wicked and the righteous in how they interact with others in their field. The instant information era of today has created an environment in which it would be difficult to not look at how others do business, yet we still fall into the trap of failing to take counsel from those around us. The picture of this verse is that of two people: one who does not learn from others and one who does.

Those who do not learn from others fall into one of two practices. We can often isolate ourselves, especially as we start to find success. When we have implemented a strategy that is working, it can be easy to stop looking outward, focusing only on our own understanding and model. This strategy is foolish and wicked, according to Solomon. He wrote to encourage us to avoid this habit of failing to learn from others. No matter how broad our knowledge base or how deep our understanding of our businesses and industry, there will always be someone more knowledgeable, someone from whom we can learn. Even the mistakes of others can teach us more about how to improve our own business.

"Where there is no guidance, a people falls,
but in an abundance of counselors there is safety."
Proverbs 11:14

It is imperative for us to look outward, and to learn from as many sources as possible. Whether we are actively seeking feedback, or simply learning from our observation of others, we cannot find success without seeking counsel. We discussed this in a previous chapter, focusing on the input and guidance of our spouse, close friends, or peers in business. Hopefully, this is something that you have already begun to practice since reading that chapter. You have those people as a springboard and as advisors to help steer you in the right direction, and it is important to continue hearing and seeking their advice. However, it is important for us to recognize the other opportunities available for us to learn.

The second practice that causes us to fail in learning from others is to look with wrong perspective or wrong motives. Though we are looking outward, we are missing what is there to learn. As we train ourselves to look outward often, looking to the successes and failures of those who are also in our industry, we should be careful to guard our thoughts and hearts. It can be easy to look outward with jealousy and frustration when we see the success of others. We are striving to find that same level of success, but instead of learning from them, we are simply brooding on the difference between their business and our own. We look to them with wisdom and with appreciation for our own business and journey, seeking to learn how to improve our own business based on what we see in theirs.

On the other hand, it can be easy to fall into a trap of pride as we observe the failures of others. The failures of others are one of the greatest ways for us to learn about our businesses. Even if we are just starting a business and have no progress or results yet, we can look to those who have failed and take careful note of what to avoid in our own work. Rather than look to them with contempt or pride, confident in our own knowledge or success, we respectfully note those things that caused them to fail. There is much to learn in failure, so we should be diligent to make the most of the struggles we see others going through.

Proverbs 3:7 and 15:33 warn us against relying on our own understanding. This is why we strive to learn from others, but even as we look to others for counsel, we must still be careful in applying the counsel given to us. We will pick up information constantly if we are vigilant in our personal and professional development. Whether passively through observation, or actively through advising, others will teach us much in life. Yet not all of the advice we receive will be good advice. This does not mean that we neglect to listen to advice that is offered to us. What it means is that we learn to apply a filter to help us discern what advice is good and godly, and what advice to ignore. This is why Solomon warned in these two verses against relying on our own understanding. Instead, he wrote that we should lean on the knowledge and wisdom of the Lord. We should allow the Holy Spirit and the Word of God to give us a greater understanding for what is truly wise and leading to righteousness, in business and in leadership.

With the discernment of God, we can learn so much from others. We can receive counsel, understand it, and apply it effectively. We can look to the wins and losses throughout our industry and gain so much information that will help us advance our own goals and causes. But we must be wise in seeking counsel, taking in knowledge, and receiving advice. Only in the wisdom of the Lord can we filter and utilize all of this information for righteous business.

Do I actively seek to learn from the successes and mistakes of others?

How often do I ask for advice?

When people give me advice, do I take it?

When I am offered advice, do I compare it with the wisdom of scriptures?

PATIENCE: RECEIVE FEEDBACK WITH GRACE

Proverbs 12:16

*"The vexation of a fool is known at once,
but the prudent ignores an insult."*

J ust as we receive counsel and advice passively, so also will we always receive feedback even when we are not looking for it. Learning to observe our peers and other businesses in our industry can keep us supplied with a steady flow of things to learn, but we all have learned by now that there will always be someone ready to give us feedback. Most people would admit that they sometimes struggle with feedback. This is something we must learn to deal with if we are to maintain positive relationships with those around us and if we are to take advantage of every opportunity to gain experience.

Feedback comes to us in many forms. It can be very subverted and reserved or it can be very brash and impactful. Feedback can be positive or negative, regardless of how it is presented to us. We should have no problem receiving valuable feedback. When people let us know that we have done a fantastic job, that they are pleased with our efforts and performance, we gladly receive it. However, when people let us know, in whatever tone of voice, that they feel as though we have not done a decent job, we often struggle to receive it well. I find this to be very intriguing. When someone tells me I have done a decent job, it is simply confirmation that I have accomplished what I set out to accomplish. Yet when someone tells me that I have not done an excellent job, no matter how hard it is to hear, they are improving my ability to do a better job on my next attempt. This is good for us, and we should receive it gladly.

Some may struggle to discern the positivity of feedback depending on how it is presented to them. Feedback that is criticism can be positive feedback. Even in being told that we have fallen short of expectations, we can be built up and encouraged. It can be easy to hear criticism and automatically categorize it as being negative, but we would be wise to learn to hear what is being said rather than how it is being said. If someone is giving us instruction on how to improve our efforts, we can grow even from a failure. This is the beauty of feedback. It is far easier to receive positive or obviously constructive feedback with grace and patience, but we can continue to develop ourselves as we learn to discern and receive feedback better each time.

Sometimes we receive negative feedback that is either harsh or unfounded. I have experienced this in my life and spent more time than I care to admit worrying about what was said to me. This is a lesson from which we must learn. As you receive negative feedback, receive it with wisdom and discernment. Receive it graciously and commit to understanding why they have given you this negative feedback. When we can learn to understand our feedback to a deeper degree, we can appreciate it better. By being careful to understand people, we can better understand what they are saying to us.

One thing we must remember when we receive negative feedback is that the person giving us this negativity is also human, just like us. They may be frustrated, going through a difficult season of life, or overly concerned about what we are trying to accomplish. When we hear this kind of negative feedback about our efforts or accomplishments, it can be easy to respond with the same negativity. If the negative feedback is given simply in poor spirit, we lower ourselves to that same level of foolishness when we respond in kind. However, I would suggest that most negative feedback is not given simply in poor spirit. It is given with good intentions but given in a way that is difficult to receive happily. Whatever the case, it is our responsibility to receive what is being given, and our prerogative to use that information appropriately.

In some cases, we may receive very mean-spirited feedback but find that there is some truth to what is being said. Our response determines whether or not we can grow even from poor feedback. In other cases, we may receive stern feedback that is very constructive, yet still difficult to digest. When we struggle with this, we have the option of asking for clarification or further detail. This is something I rarely felt comfortable doing as a young manager. I take the feedback given and figure out what to do with it. But if you do not understand or if you feel hurt, be honest with the one who gave the feedback. So long as it was not mean-spirited feedback, people will usually be happy to clarify and help you grow even more, for that is why they gave the feedback in the first place.

In some cases, you may even receive feedback that is completely unfounded. Whether based on a rumor, a misconception, or an outright lie, there will be times when someone tells how they feel about something that is not even true about us, our team, or our businesses. In these cases, it may be worth the discomfort to confront any untruths and clarify why the feedback was given. We must do this with humility and patience, however. Rather than being quick and bold to point out why the feedback is unfounded, have a private conversation with the one who gave the feedback. If you alone are being insulted or demeaned, this is not a major concern, but if your team or organization may suffer in its reputation, you may find that you need to rectify whatever has gone wrong. This must be done prayerfully and graciously.

Feedback can be a wonderful thing, but it can be difficult to manage effectively and appropriately, depending on how it is given. In all cases, we must be patient, humble, and gracious. It is foolish to respond with equal negativity when we receive demeaning feedback, but it is equally foolish to ignore any lessons that may be available to us, even in negative feedback. What we do with information determines its value. Use discernment to make the most out of all feedback you receive, ignoring insults and being thankful for constructive criticism.

What is the most recent feedback I have received?

When was the last time I asked for feedback?

How do I respond to criticism?

Am I grateful for the opportunities provided by criticism?

FEEDBACK:
CONSISTENTLY
COMMUNICATE
WITH PEERS

Proverbs 12:17

"Whoever speaks the truth gives honest evidence,
but a false witness utters deceit."

Proverbs 12:17 tells us to speak the truth, but the language used is especially important for understanding the whole context. Solomon was instructing us to breathe out truth. This is an important distinction. It is easy to speak the truth sometimes. When someone asks me about their performance, it can be easy to tell them when they are doing quite well. But when a team has failed to reach its goals, it can be extremely difficult to let them know how badly they have done. We are to breathe out truth, especially as leaders. As a leader and manager, I have the responsibility to lead those who are making work happen. If I fail to engage with them honestly on a consistent basis, they will inevitably fall short.

In the course of a workday, it can be easy to limit verbal interaction to small talk or even gossip and complaining. These things roll naturally off the tongue of every human. I have ended many days with the frustration of knowing that I was verbally unproductive, causing myself and my team to miss opportunities to make strides in reaching our goals. This can be a frustrating concept to put into practice, as it may make us feel as though we are not allowed to have small talk or share things with coworkers that are not related to work. This is not at all what I am saying. In fact, it is particularly important to have good rapport with your team members. Taking time to talk with them about their lives, their struggles at work and at home, and other "small talk" details is an important part of leading well. What I am saying is that we must build the habit of consistently giving feedback to our team. Learn to take advantage of every opportunity to communicate constructively with your team members.

The only way we can consistently communicate constructively with our team is if we learn to be vigilant in observing and leading our team. I have known managers who managed their business well by sitting in the office, understanding metrics, and giving out orders based on those metrics. This is not leadership. These managers had no relationship with their team members, and though the business was growing, the individuals were not. Rather than having the perspective of an effective manager, we should have the perspective of a powerful leader. Look at our businesses, our team, and the individuals that comprise that team with a leader's eyes. Understand what they are going through, what is affecting their performance, and what is hindering their growth. Be vigilant in observing your team and you will be properly equipped to consistently give positive feedback.

It is obvious why positive feedback is good, but consistency can be a challenge. The reason consistent feedback is good is that when we are not consistent, we are not setting a firm foundation to every step in the growth of our team. When I give a team member feedback on their performance in a certain area, they will then try to do something with that information. Having done something with it, they need to know if they have done well. They need to know where to go next. It is my job as the leader to point them in the right direction. This requires consistency. Along with this crucial aspect of effective leadership, it is a biblical command for us to help others at every opportunity.

> "So then, as we have opportunity, let us do
> good to everyone, and especially to those
> who are of the household of faith."
> Galatians 6:10

If we are to do good to everyone at every opportunity, then it is imperative for us to have consistent constructive communication with our peers and team members. Paul writes this to the church, encouraging this practice especially towards those within the church. In the context of our businesses, we can understand how much more important it is to serve our team members well at every opportunity. The best way to serve our team members is to help them grow. Do this by steering them away from their mistakes and towards better habits, more efficient work, and a clearer mindset. Whether we are communicating with fellow managers or with our followers, we must be vigilant to take advantage of every opportunity to help them in this way.

Of course, this practice will look different if we are interacting with fellow managers and leaders. We may have to be more creative in how we give them feedback. For many of us, we will find that we have to give feedback on an aspect of the business that we do not manage. Give feedback with humility, but do not be afraid to be honest. You may help your peers with an outside opinion, and they may help you understand their portion of the business better than you did before.

I cannot write enough about the importance of consistent feedback, but I encourage you to discover the benefits for yourself as you put this into practice. Your team ought to always be growing and improving, and it is up to you and your feedback to ensure that this is the case.

How much of my communication with my team involves feedback?

Can I see growth in my team?

When was the last time I chose not to give feedback?

How has feedback helped me grow?

RESERVATION: SLOW TO SPEAK, QUICK TO ENCOURAGE

Proverbs 12:18

*"There is one whose rash words are like sword thrusts,
but the tongue of the wise brings healing."*

I n learning to give consistent feedback, we hope to build habits of speaking into the lives of our followers at every single opportunity. This is extremely easy for those who are not careful about how they speak to others. I have had managers who always had something to say, but it was not always constructive or positive. This is the challenge we face as we learn to lead and as we learn to communicate consistently. We need to learn how to communicate and give feedback consistently without allowing our emotions to dictate what we say and how we say it.

Without any care for our manner of speaking, it can be extremely easy to lash out when team members fall short or when someone makes a mistake. Negativity rolls right off our tongue, as we read in a previous chapter about receiving feedback. If you have ever received negative or mean feedback, then hopefully you will understand the importance of learning to avoid doing the same to others. Though our followers can still learn from negative feedback that we give them, this is not the best way to build them up.

One key to building good habits of both self-control and consistent feedback is remembering that a leader's job is to grow the organization by growing the people that comprise the organization. Any manager can allow himself to lash out at mediocre performance or careless mistakes, but this will not grow those we lead. Outbursts may correct an error in action, but it will only hurt the one who made the error. This produces short-term results but damages our team and organization in the long run. People are the highest value assets that we have in our businesses. No matter how large or small your organization, the people that work within your organization are of more value than any other asset and even any amount of profit. Grow your people and watch them grow your business.

This verse has a bit of contrast in comparison with the idea of learning to "breathe out truth" in the previous verse. Do we always give feedback, or do we give feedback only when we are able to do so without accidentally being negative or demeaning? The answer to that question is yes, but it forces us to consider our own personal and professional development. As we learn to control our emotions, giving feedback objectively and kindly, we may find that we have to delay in communicating with a team member who has caused us some frustration or set back. As we learn to speak positively and objectively, we can see those things that need to be addressed and understand not only how they affect the business, but also how they affect the individual in which we see them. When I encounter a team member who has let down the team because of laziness or negligence, I want to correct those things in that team member primarily for their own sake, not the sake of the business. Their laziness may set the team back today, but laziness will continue to set that team member back for their entire life if we are not bold enough, honest enough, and objective enough to address this change that needs to be made.

If I am unable to do this in a kind way, it is important for me to wait to have that conversation. It is better to delay in giving feedback than to be hasty in hurting a team member. Any time I have ever failed in giving feedback without emotional clouding, I have insulted or hurt team members, damaging the rapport I had with them. This sets our own leadership back, and it sets the development of the team and team members back. An important part of developing this habit of giving consistent feedback that is not altered by my own emotions is to take time to understand anything that contributed to the inferior performance or mistake that is generating my feedback. Why did my team member fail or fall short? Why has this happened and what can be done about it? This helps us address the issue with an individual more objectively and with a deeper understanding of what happened.

The way that we speak with our team members ought always to have a healing, growing effect. When we lash out, we are not only offending and hurting the team members now, but we are also leaving scars that will distort any future interaction or feedback. Our words carry great weight, especially as leaders. Always favor a slow reaction over a hurtful one. Though we ought to give feedback as quickly as possible to prevent further mistakes, do not let your poor feedback be the next mistake that happens for your team member.

Is my feedback consistently positive, or do I allow myself to give reactionary feedback?

Do I give feedback that grows people or grows business?

How can I build habits to always give positive feedback?

TRUTHFULNESS: EVEN WHEN IT HURTS, HONESTY IS GOOD BUSINESS

Proverbs 12:19

"Truthful lips endure forever,
but a lying tongue is but for a moment."

Honesty is difficult. We have discussed the importance of consistent constructive communication and, last chapter, discussed one of the things that can keep us from having this kind of habitual positive feedback in our leadership. Allowing our emotions to prod us into lashing out hurts our team and hinders the development of our good habits. However, our emotions can cause us to react in the opposite way to our team members, as well. I do not think that any leader would tell their team that everything is going great when the team is actually failing, but when we fail to tell the team the truth, we are lying to them.

Honesty can often hurt right away. It can be uncomfortable, divisive, and scary. The alternative is far worse, however. When we are not honest with our team, they will continue to fall short of expectations. When we are not honest with ourselves, we will continue to fail in developing ourselves and our businesses. But because of the difficulties inherent with total honesty, it can be easy to avoid the conversation altogether. We put off being honest and fail to give any kind of feedback whatsoever. No news is not good news in leadership and business.

Team members with whom we are not honest may never really know if they are doing a bad job. Even if it seems obvious to us, their leader, they may fail to realize that they are falling short. If they do see their shortcomings, they may fail to understand the reason for those shortcomings. We have to be honest with them in order for them to have a chance at improving. I have found that the hardest things to be honest with team members about are the trivial things. Their performance may be okay, but they are failing to follow proper procedures as they do their work. Avoiding addressing these issues may seem insignificant to us as leaders, but it is our responsibility to be honest about even those trivial things. Team members look to us for guidance. Though they may sometimes still have resentment towards us for our honesty, they will benefit from it and look back with thankfulness. I can say this from experience as both a leader and a follower.

We must be honest with ourselves, as well as with others. Honestly assess your own performance, the health of your business, and your own development over time. You may be the most difficult person with whom you have to be honest. In my own personal and professional development, honesty is what has helped me make the most crucial decisions. Choices in my education, career, and personal life have happened only as a result of being honest with myself. We cannot effectively grow and grow others if we are not first honest with ourselves. What do we enjoy? What is difficult for us? What do we most want to do? What is most important to us? Even in the context of our businesses, the honest answers to these questions shape our perspective, define our ambitions, and write our story.

> "Faithful are the wounds of a friend;
> profuse are the kisses of an enemy."
> Proverbs 27:6

Making honesty a habit is less difficult the longer you work at that habit. When we decide to start being honest with our followers about their performance, they may feel as though we are attacking them, trying to hurt them or tear them down. Pointing out their deficient performance or bad attitudes may cause them to feel as though you are picking on them. However, you know that you are trying to help them, and as their leader, you can see the big picture that you are trying to work towards. As you continue to be consistently honest with them, they will come to understand this, and you will be able to be their partner in their own journey to excellence and success. I have had team members who experienced frustration with me as I was honest with them, yet later received thanks from them for the encouragement to be better. Honesty is one of the most powerful tools that a leader can use.

Dishonesty is easy, and avoidance of honesty is even easier, but we cannot allow these to become our habits. To lie or avoid the truth may be comfortable in the moment, but that moment is only one moment.

The impact that it can have is far longer than we imagine in that single moment. I can think back to team members with whom I struggled to be honest, and I know that they are worse off as individuals than if I had done my job as their leader correctly. It was easy to avoid being honest with them, but their team suffered as a result. If we are thinking long-term, we understand the gravity of a moment of honesty versus a moment of dishonesty.

Be honest with team members about their performance. Be honest with yourself about your own performance. Be honest with your team about the business. Honesty will go a long way in building rapport, maintaining vision and growth, and creating value far beyond any numbers or metrics.

Am I committed to my business and team enough to be honest with them?

Do I care enough about my team to keep them from falling?

Do I value success more than I value comfort?

PLANNING:
FAIL TO PLAN,
PLAN TO FAIL

Proverbs 12:20

*"Deceit is in the heart of those who devise evil,
but those who plan peace have joy."*

So far in this book, we have discussed what it looks like to practice righteous business. The righteous businessperson does not plan evil, as Proverbs 12:20 describes, but that does not mean that a well-intentioned plan cannot lead to evil. Solomon warns against the plans of an evil person, and I would caution that even the righteous person should learn to plan in such a way that those plans cannot lead to a less than righteous outcome. We should plan above reproach. We do this by ensuring that there is no part of our plan that involves any kind of deceit or deceitful motive and being detailed enough in our plans to anticipate any obstacles we may face.

Instead of wicked plans, we are encouraged to make righteous plans because those plans lead to peace and joy. What is inherent in this verse is that we are making plans. We are not being instructed to plan because it is assumed that we are already planning. We cannot be successful in business if we do not plan. I once had a market manager who regularly reminded me that failing to plan is planning to fail. It was an annoying reminder, but a very necessary one. Some may feel that planning is a tricky subject, in light of what James 4:13-17 says. We should not make assumptions about our plans, but this does not mean that we should not plan.

Proverbs 19:21 tells us that we have many plans, but it is the Lord's will that prevails. This implies, along with Proverbs 12:20, that we should make plans! The challenge is making plans that are aligned with God's will for our lives and our businesses. We can look back to Romans 12:2, referenced many times throughout this book, and be reminded of the necessity for a Christian, manager or otherwise, to learn to discern the will of God. As we learn to make good plans for our businesses, we cannot neglect to ensure that those plans are in line with the will of God. When we fail to check our plans against the will of God, through prayer and good counsel, we make plans that fall short of righteous business.

Many managers fail to plan as a consistent part of their leadership. They may recognize certain times when a particular season or event requires planning ahead, but their daily schedule does not consist of planning. This causes us to miss the peace and joy mentioned in today's verse. How can we have peace and joy in our businesses, regardless of any obstacles or challenges we face? By knowing and trusting a well-made, righteous plan. Managers of distinct levels within an organization have different obligations regarding planning, but all managers must plan. Typically, the higher in the organization a manager operates, the more long-term his plans must be. For the front-line manager, his plans may focus on the current day and week, while his manager may plan with next month and next quarter in mind. In either scenario, planning is necessary for the success of the business.

Every manager experiences obstacles to making planning a regular part of their schedules, but every manager should work to eliminate those obstacles and instill good habits of planning. We often can get caught up in tasks that can be delegated, feeling as though we have to be more involved in the work that is happening. The closer a manager is to the labor being done, the more prone he will be to this obstacle. Another distraction is putting out relational fires among our team members, allowing ourselves to get too caught up with personal issues between two individuals on our team. These, and many other, problems waste time that we could spend on planning.

The problem with tending to these obstacles, which are real problems and challenges for our team, is that it keeps us from planning to resolve those problems and the things that caused those problems. When we allow ourselves to be distracted by our team's problems of today, we cannot make plans to overcome those problems tomorrow. If we are shorthanded today because of staffing problems, we could fill that staffing need ourselves, or we could plan to resolve staffing problems for the rest of the week and month. This is how we access peace and joy through good planning. We may experience discomfort today, but our planning will allow us to experience great improvements within our work environment and business. This also provides greater peace and joy for our team members on a more long-term basis than if we were to simply help them today.

It can be easy to get so caught up in right now that we fail to plan for later. Similarly, it can be so easy to get caught up in planning from our own wisdom and understanding that we fail to plan according to the unfailing wisdom and purpose of God. In order to do righteous business, we have to become proficient at planning. We must plan consistently, evaluate our plans consistently, and seek feedback on our plans consistently. It is much easier to solve a problem by tackling it head on today, but the solution will only be a short-term solution. Righteous business requires that we have the wisdom and maturity to develop a long-term solution to the problems that we are facing. This has the most benefit for our followers, customers, and organization as a whole.

Do I plan consistently?

What things keep me from planning successfully?

What struggles or failures have I experienced recently that I could have defeated through consistent planning?

How have I experienced peace as a result of good planning in the past?

When has my team experienced difficulty because I failed to plan?

FAILURES: SETBACKS ARE NOT FAILURES

Proverbs 12:21

*"No ill befalls the righteous,
but the wicked are filled with trouble."*

Failures exist. It seems necessary to start this chapter with a sort of disclaimer. Even the righteous can stray far enough from the path of righteousness to see their business venture fail. However, in the vast majority of cases, this is not what we experience. It is important to point out that we are not guaranteed success simply because of our label, whether we label ourselves or are labeled by others. We can and will make mistakes, but we must learn to have the right perspective on the results of those mistakes.

Whenever we make mistakes and things do not go as planned or as hoped, we experience setbacks. Setbacks are those circumstances that lie between us and our goals. Hindrances that arise as a result of our poor planning, our wrong choices, and even various external factors are temporary events in our lives. Every single one of us will experience these setbacks, but we must learn to manage them properly if we are to continue to make progress towards our goals. The difference between a setback and a failure is our perspective. When we are able to get back up, it is only a setback. When we can still see our future filled with success, it is only a setback. Many people allow setbacks to weigh them down to a greater extent than they would if they had a more positive attitude. By having a positive attitude about our goals, progress, and even setbacks, we can overcome even the greatest negative circumstances.

Proverbs 12:21 is a promise to us that no ill will befall us as we strive to do righteous business. Romans 8:28 tells us that all things work for our good, because God calls us to do what we are doing. It is because of these promises that we are able to view setbacks as the temporary events that they really are. Because of God's promises to us, we can get back up with the confidence we need to reach our goals. This is where the difference between setbacks and failures are seen. When we allow ourselves to focus on the current negative situation, we forget about the future success that we can experience if we continue to strive for righteousness and excellence. Our focus and perspective allow us to access the promises made to us by God.

This is not a "name it, claim it" message of making a way for ourselves by our attitude, or glossing over the reality of mistakes and setbacks. One of the most commonly referred to verses in scripture regarding success is Jeremiah 29:11. God has plans for us, and those plans are good. God desires us to be successful. But when God spoke through Jeremiah to tell the Israelites of His plan for them, it was while they were in exile in Babylon. They were in exile because of their own mistakes, but God still had a future of hope and success for them. We can learn from this example as we navigate our setbacks in striving for righteous business.

The Israelites were in exile, but they still had a future of hope in God. However, God required that they work to improve on their mistakes, telling them in the very next verse the actions needed for them to come out of exile and experience the fullness of His plan for their success and joy. God told them to pray, to seek Him, to change their ambitions and perspectives, and by this to overcome setbacks. Had the Israelites ignored this warning and command, they would have experienced failure and continued to live in exile. We experience the same thing in our righteous business. By focusing on the future that we are promised in pursuing righteousness, we can overcome the setbacks that we experience as a result of our mistakes.

This chapter has addressed mistakes and setbacks as though they are inevitable. If this is frustrating to you, you must be new to business, management, and righteousness. Welcome to the team! We, like Paul, are pressing on towards the goal of the upward calling in Christ Jesus (Philippians 3:14), but we, like Paul, are not perfect. We will undoubtedly experience setbacks as we make mistakes and learn how to do business righteously. It is important to remember that everyone makes mistakes, everyone experiences setbacks, and those who have the right perspective will overcome. This attitude will give us the capacity to get back up and tackle the results of our mistakes with confidence and joy.

What was the last setback I experienced?

Do I view setbacks as temporary hindrances or as hard failures?

How do I respond to setbacks in my business?

How can I change my perspective to be more focused on future successes than current setbacks?

ACTIONS:
ACT THE TRUTH

Proverbs 12:22

*"Lying lips are an abomination to the Lord,
but those who act faithfully are his delight."*

We have learned to be careful about what we say and how we say it, but the way we act reveals more truth than the way we speak. It is certainly true that actions speak louder than words, especially when we are in a position of leadership or management. Even for the entrepreneur with no employees, there are many people watching you carefully, judging whether or not they can trust you and your business. Within your organization, there are many people observing, comparing your words against your actions. Do you abide by the things you speak to them?

Most of us try to believe what we tell our followers, and some of us might think we are in complete agreement with the things we speak. The fact is many people feel a certain way about their business or organization, but speak differently about it to their followers. If the business is experiencing a slump, we want to maintain good morale. We speak encouragingly to our followers and team members, but inside, we feel frustrated or defeated. In some cases, our team members may feel frustration with another manager or leader in the organization, and we feel the same way! But we understand that we have a responsibility to speak positively about the leadership of our organization, so we pretend to like our boss more than we do. Acting differently than we speak is a common and very detrimental problem for us as we do business.

Followers recognize when our words and actions do not match. I have often felt that I could get away with speaking differently than I feel, but my team members always knew when I could not abide by what I was saying. Your team members are the same way. Facial expressions, tone of voice, work ethic, and overall demeanor tells followers all they need to know. Resolving this issue in our leadership can be very difficult but failing to reconcile our words and actions can hurt us and our businesses greatly. Learning to articulate how we feel to our followers and peers takes much practice, but it is worth the effort. This involves much personal and professional development. By learning to be more aware of our actions, how we are working, we can begin to change our demeanor and make our words and actions match. Some examples that I have experienced in my own management include my determination to meet a goal that I communicated to my team, my reaction to changes within the organization, my energy levels as I conducted my work, and my commitment to winning the day.

Another consideration in acting truthfully involves the idea of being two-faced. We may adopt this practice as a way to get along with people, seeking to avoid conflict. We may act this way to avoid difficult conversations. This is much easier in the short-term but will hurt our businesses in the long-run. We need to learn to have the confidence to be honest and upfront with people about how we feel. Whether this means being honest with our team members about their performance or attitude or being honest with our managers about directions or goals that they are giving. Honesty, humility, and tactfulness are key to helping you act truthfully in these situations.

Proverbs 12:22 says that we must act faithfully, and so far, we have discussed the importance of ensuring that our words and actions match within the context of our businesses and management. This also includes the faith that we proclaim. Even in an organization that prohibited religious discussions, my team knew what I believed. If we truly desire to conduct righteous business, we must act righteously in our businesses. Thankfully, my team members did not expect me to be perfect, but they certainly expected me to act according to the faith that I proclaimed. In some cases, this meant acting in opposition to what was expected of me, but in other cases it meant going beyond what was expected of me. In all situations, acting according to my faith meant treating people differently than they expected to be treated by a manager. I still stay connected with people that I have led in previous roles, and one of the things they mention most in comparing following me versus following subsequent managers is the way I treated them. Our faith, in pursuing righteous business, requires that we adhere to strict principles, even as we work.

Acting truthfully is harder than just speaking truthfully, but it is just as important. The two notions lie on either side of the same coin of honesty and integrity. By learning to always reconcile the way we feel and the way we speak, we will find ourselves in difficult positions, but when managed correctly, those positions will always gain us respect with our followers and peers. Let your pursuit of righteous business dictate your actions and words, and you will learn to act faithfully, according to Proverbs.

Do I recognize when my words and actions do not match?

When was the last time my followers pointed out a difference between my words and actions?

When was the last time I struggled with acting according to my faith within my business?

How can I learn to be more aware of how my actions reveal my feelings?

ACUMEN: EXPERTISE REQUIRES CONSTANT GROWTH

Proverbs 12:23

*"A prudent man conceals knowledge,
but the heart of fools proclaims folly."*

An expert is someone who is skilled and knowledgeable in their field. We can become experts in our businesses through practice, but we must continue practicing in order to remain experts. Expertise requires constant growth. In striving for righteous business, it is inherent that we become experts in our businesses and industry. If we fail to develop our knowledge and our skills, we will not be able to be successful. Proverbs 12:23 speaks to this accumulation and appropriation of knowledge.

Reading this verse, we can see that Solomon wrote with the assumption that the reader is knowledgeable. It would be foolish to think of oneself as a leader or manager and not have any knowledge or skills pertinent to the organization in which we operate. The assumption that we are knowledgeable is a challenge. It is important for us to assess our expertise on a regular basis. This is part of becoming an expert. Not only should we know all about our own business, but we should know about our entire industry. Pay attention to your industry, the things that affect your industry, and the events that are happening within your industry. Though external, what is happening in your industry is happening to your business. Without a broad knowledge of what affects your business, you cannot plan and lead your business successfully.

Within your own business, there will be job roles that you have never held. It is important that you understand these jobs. Even if you only spend a day learning about one job role, your ability to lead those who perform that job will increase significantly. By understanding the parts that make up the whole, you will continue developing your expertise. This can be a challenge for someone who leads an exceptionally large team or operates within a very diverse organization, but the time invested in understanding every detail will strengthen your ability to understand the relationship between every part of your business. In some cases, it will be difficult or impossible to learn every job role in its entirety. For instance, the Human Resource Manager may not feasibly be able to learn how to develop software or engineer hardware. However, learning the connection between the various inputs and outputs of the business will enable the Human Resource Manager to better understand the business's staffing needs.

Having gained knowledge about our businesses and industry, we need to learn to use it appropriately. This is why connecting the dots between various job roles is so important. Using our expertise appropriately also means understanding how to share our knowledge. The phrase used in Proverbs 12:23, that we should conceal knowledge, refers both to storing up knowledge as well as not bragging or blurting everything we know inappropriately. No matter how much of an expert we are, it is of no benefit to be arrogant in sharing our knowledge. Our expertise is always especially useful to us, but it is only useful to others when we share it at the right times and in the right ways. We may try to teach a team member something new, but if we are arrogant in the way that we teach, we are hurting our team members. We may try to share some new knowledge with a peer in our industry, but if we are bragging about how much we know, we are hurting our relationship with them. It is prudent to conceal our expertise until just the right time. This is an important part of being an effective expert.

Our followers can help us as we develop our expertise. Most managers, no matter how long they have been in the business, have at least one follower who has an equal or greater tenure. However, because that follower is not a manager, they have a more specific job role, which means that they have more direct experience in a particular aspect of the business. We have to be humble enough to learn from them. Whether they give us suggestions, point out obstacles, or confront mistakes, our followers can be a huge asset to us as we strive to increase our knowledge. Even newer team members have different perspectives and backgrounds that can prove useful to us as we learn all that we can. Pay attention to your team members' knowledge just as much as you pay attention to your business, and you will gain ground in becoming an expert.

Expertise is necessary in business. As we learn more about our businesses, our desire to learn even more should grow. No one ever became an expert and then stopped learning. The greatest minds throughout history continued pursuing a deeper knowledge until their death bed. It should be the same with us, not only because we have a passion for our businesses, but also because we owe it to our followers. Our followers look up to us because we are supposed to guide them. We cannot guide them if we are not continuing to grow in our own knowledge and understanding. As you lead your team and manage your business, always be moving forward. Deepen your understanding of your business, broaden your knowledge of your industry, and become more of an expert every day.

Am I an expert in my field?

What habits do I already have to develop my expertise?

When have I shared my expertise in arrogance?

Do I allow my followers to help me become more of an expert?

LEADERSHIP: DILIGENCE DEVELOPS LEADERS

Proverbs 12:24

*"The hand of the diligent will rule,
while the slothful will be put to forced labor."*

Diligence has been an underlying theme throughout this book, but as we draw to the close of Proverbs 12, diligence becomes more prominent in the discussion. As we strive for righteous business, it is inherent that we are diligent. Arduous work, excellent work, and purposeful work are all a key part of conducting business in a way that is righteous. When we fail to work with excellence, we cannot say that our business is righteous. However, this does not mean that a lack of diligence means a lack of work. As Proverbs 12:24 points out, even the lazy person must work, albeit a different kind of work.

By doing work well, we will eventually excel in what we are doing. If you are an employee, working under a manager or management team, your diligence will not go unnoticed. Excellent work will stand out from the rest of the work being done. Though we know that life "isn't fair," it is understood that diligent work leads to greater reward, in every circumstance. Typically, we experience that reward through raises or promotions. Aside from the formal rewards offered within business for excellent work, the natural result of diligent work is that we change our own status within our businesses. Today's verse declares that the diligent person will find themselves in a position of leadership.

Management teams should always be thinking of succession planning. Even if they do not foresee needing to fill a gap in management anytime soon, succession planning is a natural part of leading and managing a team of people. A good manager is always observing, making note of which team members would make good leaders. By committing to work with diligence, we highlight ourselves as the natural choice in our managers' succession planning. Another advantage we have as diligent workers is that we are looked up to by our peers and can be a help to management by guiding those with whom we work. Part of diligent work is contributing to our team.

In some cases, the diligent worker will find themselves in a very informal position of leadership when formal leadership is poor or not present. In my own experience, I was recently out of work for two weeks due to illness, leaving my team without any oversight. In our very high-volume environment, this was a setup for failure. However, one of my best team members, without being told or asked, began calling the shots. She understands the business well and has since been promoted, having the confidence to lead others. In my absence, she carried the team through my unexpected absence and earned herself an incredible new position of leadership with the company.

As we experience this natural progression for ourselves, we should keep in mind what Jesus explained to the Sons of Thunder in Matthew 20. James and John asked for a position of leadership and authority in the Kingdom of Heaven, but Jesus made it clear that the righteous do not practice leadership in the same way that the unrighteous do. Rather than lead in pride and arrogance, we lead in humility, gratitude, and love. We lead others by serving them and building them up. We lead others by doing what is best for them, no matter how uncomfortable it is for us or for them. Often, this takes greater diligence than leading pridefully. Taking the time to care for those we are leading, understanding their strengths and weaknesses, supporting them in their struggles, and pushing them past their fears; this is truly diligent leadership.

If you are already in a position of management, this chapter is still for you. Unless you are the top leader within your organization, you are still a follower to some other leader. Work diligently, excelling in what you do, so that you can earn even greater influence from which to practice righteous business. If you are the top leader in your organization, or are an entrepreneur running your own business, you have a community you serve and an industry in which you operate. Work diligently for the sake of those who are looking to you for an example or for encouragement. Work diligently even for those who look in envy at your success. Because you are already in a position of leadership and prominence, you have that much more responsibility to work with diligence.

Whatever your position, do the work you do with diligence, understanding that it is not for power, position, or wealth that you must work diligently. You should work diligently for the opportunity to edify others and glorify God. This is why we do righteous business. Be diligent so you can be righteous, and by doing so, you will be successful in whatever business you do.

Is my work diligent, according to what the Bible says is diligent?

What leadership do I hold in my business?

How do I lead others? In arrogance, or in love?

In what ways can I improve my work ethic so that I can be a better leader and influence for righteousness in business?

ANXIETY: HEAR A GOOD WORD, SPEAK A GOOD WORD

Proverbs 12:25

*"Anxiety in a man's heart weighs him down,
but a good word makes him glad."*

Anyone focused on accomplishing something great will have great concern for it. This concern can turn into anxiety if we are not careful. Quickly, anxiety becomes a distraction, keeping us from thinking clearly about our task. In business, this is especially true, more so for the managers of a business. As the manager, it is our responsibility to ensure the continued growth and success of the business, which requires much of our attention. Left unchecked, this attention can cause us to live with stress and anxiety.

Anxiety affects us in many ways, but in every way, it is unhealthy. A certain level of stress may become normal for most managers, depending on the nature of your business, but this stress is never good for us. I often struggle to balance apathy and extreme anxiety when I think about my business. I either have no concern whatsoever, or I have insomnia as a result of my unhealthy concern. This is why it is so important for us to learn how to defeat anxiety as we strive to do good business. If we were to build the most successful business in the world, but allowed ourselves to live with crippling anxiety, it would be difficult to say that we are doing business righteously. Righteous business requires a proper perspective and prioritization of our businesses, our lives, and our goals. Anxiety hampers our prioritization.

Proverbs 12:25 gives us the solution to the anxiety that is building up within us: to hear a good word. This can be understood in a number of ways, but the goal of hearing a good word is to receive instruction, encouragement, advice, and other such things that can keep our mindset positive and growing. There are a number of great ways for us to regularly hear a good word, and this is something that we should make into a habit. Rather than going to a source of good words when we are struggling with anxiety, we should add these sources into our regular schedule as a way of continuing to be uplifted and guided in our success. Consistency is one of the strongest points of this practice.

One of the main ways that we can hear a good word on a consistent basis is through podcasts. We live in a time that allows us such ease of access to wonderful resources, and we should take full advantage of that. Take time this week to find podcasts that speak about business, leadership, creativity, ingenuity, and other things that can strengthen your leadership and management. These can be an encouragement to you, but they should also challenge you to continue in your personal and professional development. From Craig Groeschel to Simon Sinek to your local church pastor, there are countless opportunities available for you to consistently listen to a good word.

Our friendships are another source of good words for us as we work to keep anxiety at bay. We have discussed this in a previous chapter but should not overlook the power of an outside perspective, especially of someone who is very close to us. By sharing our frustrations and concerns with friends who are willing to listen, we can gain valuable advice and priceless encouragement. We need this fellowship, even with people who are not in business with us, in order to stay motivated in the face of challenges and struggles.

Feedback from our customers and team members is a scary way to hear a good word, but it is an excellent way, nonetheless. In seeking feedback, another thing discussed previously in this book, we will hear both positive and negative feedback. However, both forms of feedback can still be a good word for us. Positive feedback is a relief, letting us know what we are doing well and reminding us of our success so far. Negative feedback is a revelation of the opportunities we have for improvement. Personally, anxiety comes most often in the face of ambiguity or uncertainty. Negative feedback is often very direct in addressing what went wrong. This helps us clarify how to move forward, even better than we were before.

The last source of good words that should be noted is books. This source is similar to podcasts, as there are countless books available for us to read and treasure. Many people in today's podcast world struggle to make reading a habit, but reading is beneficial in many ways beyond just the information contained within each book. The act of reading forces us to take our attention off those things that are causing us anxiety. Sitting still and concentrating on the words on every page can do wonders for clearing our minds. Out of all the books available for us to read, the Bible should be our number one. We cannot do righteous business if we have no understanding of what righteousness looks like. This book is intended to help define righteous business for the reader but is only a shadow of its source. God's Word should be our primary source of good words in our daily routine. Without the source of Truth and goodness, we cannot make the most of any other source of good words we find.

Just as we experience anxiety, we know that there are those around us who also have the same struggle. As we learn to defeat anxiety, we should help our team members and peers do the same. We can be a source of good words for those with whom we interact on a regular basis. Everything we learn can be shared with those around us to keep them from being hindered by anxiety in their lives. A simple encouragement can go a long way in keeping someone on track as they also strive to do righteous business. In your battle against anxiety, learn to recognize those battling around you, and take time to give them an assist.

Learn to give careful thought to your business without developing fear or an unhealthy obsession. This is the balance we must find as we give our best to our businesses. We will fail in this balancing act, and this is when anxiety creeps in. Righteous business is challenging, but we have the support we need, to a greater extent today than ever available before. When we battle anxiety, we must remember the words and promises of God.

> "Whatever is true, whatever is honorable, whatever
> is just, whatever is pure, whatever is lovely, whatever
> is commendable, if there is any excellence, if there is
> anything worthy of praise, think about these things."
> Philippians 4:8

Do I let my concern for my business become anxiety?

How do I overcome my anxiety?

What habits do I have to regularly hear a good word?

How can I help those around me overcome their anxiety?

NEIGHBORING:
BE A GOOD
NEIGHBOR

Proverbs 12:26

"One who is righteous is a guide to his neighbor,
but the way of the wicked leads them astray."

As we learn to be encouraging to those in business around us, we also should make effective use of our experience and expertise by supporting our neighbors in business. It is one thing to be friendly and casually supportive, but as people doing righteous business, we should go beyond the expected and normal. Counter to the typical ways of thinking about competition in business, we should support other leaders, managers, and entrepreneurs in our community and industry. Competition is a good thing, but eternal success is better.

In order to learn to support those around us, we have to learn to be aware of them. Though we may not know their numbers or understand their specific vision, we can get a general idea of how well they are doing by observing, and also by being friendly to them. In saying that we should be friendly with our neighbors, I am not saying that we have to add all of our neighbors as friends on social media, have weekend get-togethers, and go to the movies. What I am saying is that we pay attention to their progress, their demeanor, and their work ethic. As competition, we should be paying attention to them anyway, but as friendly competition, we should pay attention with care and empathy. When we perceive that they are struggling, it is our responsibility to offer them support in any way that we can, even if they are our "competition." The race that we are running is a race in which we can all earn our prize, contrary to the race of this world.

Competition can and should be fierce in every industry. If there is no competition, there is no progress. As we work to become more efficient, our neighbors will also become more efficient. As we advance our technology, techniques, and outputs, our neighbors will do the same. This is what drives a good economy, but it will suffer when businesses are not competing fairly within an industry. Along with sharing encouragement, we can share advice with our neighbors. We can let them in on those things that we have learned to be an immense help to our businesses' development. In our personal development as leaders, we can build up other leaders by sharing our experiences.

Even our mistakes are made much more valuable when we share what we learned from them with others in business with us.

Some of our neighbors may be uncomfortable with this idea. Sure, they are happy to take whatever advice or support you give them, but this practice is so contrary to the way the world does business that our neighbors may not want to reciprocate your support. Beyond just encouraging words, we may be the only one in our community or industry willing to share what we are learning and what is helping us be successful. This is okay. We cannot expect that people who are not striving to practice righteous business will practice righteous business. Many people may even think that we are foolish for being so open with what is leading us to success, but they will undoubtedly hear what we have to say, understanding that it will be a benefit to them. Either way, we can expect them to eventually see the benefits of doing business according to the example we are setting. We should be patient, persevering in our willingness to be a good neighbor to those around us. It will pay off! We will contribute to a community of people committed to each other's success, and everyone will be better for it.

With that being said, some of our neighbors will decide to take advantage of the support we are giving. Rather than reciprocate, they will take our support and use it to be overly competitive against us and against others. This is to be expected in the world, and we need discernment to avoid falling into this trap. Our default attitude should be to support every neighbor around us, but we will learn to recognize when people are accepting that support with a particularly unrighteous attitude. Jesus speaks of these kinds of people in Matthew 7:6 when He warns us not to throw pearls before pigs. This is a tricky situation in which we will sometimes find ourselves, but we can overcome even unhealthy competition. With humility and wisdom, we can continue supporting others around us while politely avoiding interactions with those who have taken advantage of the help that we have given.

Helping our neighbors should be a part of what it means for us to practice righteous business. We should take every opportunity to help those around us, whether they are struggling or not. Offering a hand to those who have fallen is honorable and appreciated by all, but to offer advice or support to someone who is doing fine is unexpected. We should desire more than just to see our neighbors not fall. We should desire to see them excel, and we should help them excel with us.

Do I know who my neighbors are?

How have I helped my neighbors recently?

How can I help my neighbors today?

Am I able to discern when I should not give advice or other support to overly competitive or unrighteous neighbors?

RESOURCES: EVERY RESOURCE IS A BLESSING

Proverbs 12:27

*"Whoever is slothful will not roast his game,
but the diligent man will get precious wealth."*

B y now, we should recognize that God has abundantly blessed us. In doing business, we all have resources, time, success, and many other things that have been granted to us by God's grace and goodness. In reading Proverbs 12:27, we are challenged with the notion that some people fail to make use of the blessings that they have. This verse is what convicted and challenged me to author this entire book. The education, experience, and wisdom that I have gained up to this point in my life have been given to me by God, and I now have a responsibility to use them to edify others and glorify Him.

The picture painted by Solomon in this verse is one of a hunter who has successfully killed game and is now able to bring meat home for his family. Yet Solomon wrote that the lazy person does not cook the meat for his family. No matter his success in hunting, he has failed to experience all of the benefits of that hunt until he uses what he has gained. At the end of this chapter, we will briefly mention the benefits of the hunt aside from the game that the hunter has killed.

Each of us has this same responsibility. We may feel as though we are not very blessed, but even the time you are spending reading this book is a blessing. The air you are breathing is a blessing. Every success in your business is a blessing. We owe it to God to maximize the fruits of those blessings. It can be easy to view the blessings we have received from God as fruits for us to enjoy, but they are really seeds for us to sow. We cannot experience the fullness of our blessings until we have invested them, multiplied them, and shared them in every way that we can.

Whether it is time, talents, or treasures, it is important for us to be aware of our blessings. Only when we are aware of our blessings are we able to be thankful for them, as well as utilize them appropriately. It can be easy to focus on only the major blessings that we experience in life, neglecting to appreciate or utilize the common, subtle, and every-day blessings. Our great victories or breakthroughs as leaders, huge wins in our businesses, major goals reached in a quarter or year; these are worth celebrating and using to continue our development, but the little blessings are worth no less. Every day, we should recognize and plan to utilize the small blessings of the time that we have, the skills that we have developed, the experiences we have gained, and the wealth we have earned.

Using our blessings to the fullest requires diligence, just as leading our businesses to success requires diligence. We must be diligent in counting our blessings, diligent in investing our blessings, and even diligent in sharing our blessings. However, what we need to understand is that diligence is, itself, a blessing. Anyone can work hard, but we need God to produce good fruit as a result of our hard work. In John 15, Jesus makes one of His "I Am" statements and tells His disciples that unless they abide in Him, they cannot bear good fruit. It is important for us to remember this as we strive to practice righteous business. Once we have counted our blessings and are determined to multiply them, we must rely on the strength, wisdom, and guidance of God, through His Holy Spirit, if we are to produce good fruit from the blessings He has planted in us.

As we do business, we will encounter many successful people who are not practicing righteous business. This can be frustrating to us because we know that we are working differently for a reason, yet we desire to have that same short-term success. What we must remember is that we are building a long-term, eternal success. God has promised an abundant life to us as we live and work in accordance with His will, but the majority of the return on our investments in life will be experienced in eternity. Our diligence will pay off here, but even the greatest success here on earth cannot compare with the treasures we are storing up for ourselves in Heaven. Do not be discouraged by what you perceive as success in the lives of others. Invest, multiply, and share your blessings with diligence, and reap a harvest of even greater blessing.

The hunter who has gone out to hunt has already earned a great blessing, even before he is successful in his hunt. This is a blessing that we often overlook. By being faithful with our resources, even just our time or skills, we are inherently multiplying them. The hunter is becoming a better hunter, a better provider, a better father and husband, just by going out to hunt. Remember this as you strive for success in practicing righteous business.

If we are going to use our blessings to the full extent, we need to be experts in our trade and business, and we have to have a keen eye for every opportunity to utilize our blessings. As you develop these skills, remember to be grateful for your blessings. Increase your blessings and the blessings of others by being diligent with them, and watch your business grow in success.

When was the last time I counted my blessings?

What habits do I have to multiply my blessings?

Has there ever been a time when I worked hard, but struggled to bear good fruit?

How do I know if I am using my blessings to their full extent?

RIGHTEOUSNESS: RIGHTEOUS BUSINESS REQUIRES RIGHTEOUS LIVING

Proverbs 12:28

*"In the path of righteousness is life,
and in its pathway there is no death."*

U p until now, this book has focused primarily on what it looks like to practice righteous business. The way we conduct our business is of the utmost importance, and we have a responsibility to do good business. We have discussed habits, mindsets, and other aspects of being better leaders, better managers, and better businesspeople. At times, we have strayed into the personal aspects of righteousness, but in this last chapter, we will focus on our personal righteousness.

It would be far easier for me to author a book that does not address or challenge your personal life. If I were to have focused only on the way you behave "at work," I could have written nearly the same book. Chances are that this book would be more popular without this last chapter. However, in order to be righteous in our businesses, we have to be righteous in our personal lives. It is impossible to practice righteous business without practicing righteous living. This may be offensive or challenging to some, but it is the hard truth. Righteousness is not a business technique or strategy. In fact, according to the way the world says we should do business, some of the righteous practices advised in this book are contrary to how business should be done. Righteousness is a lifestyle, and it should permeate every aspect of our lives, our relationships, our goals, and our businesses. We cannot have an unrighteous life and a righteous business. Similarly, we cannot claim to have a righteous life if we do not have a righteous business.

> "Blessed are they who observe justice,
> who do righteousness at all times!"
> Psalm 106:3

Righteousness at all times can be a challenge, but that is why I have referred to it as a practice throughout the book. We have to practice righteousness if we are to be righteous. As Christians, we are clothed in the righteousness of Christ, but our lives should be defined by our sanctification. We cannot be sanctified in life yet not in business. We must allow ourselves to be changed in the way we live and conduct business so that we are more like Christ. Jesus may not have had a business or managed a company while He was on earth, but He left us examples of what good leadership and management looks like. We are to practice those things, following His example as we grow in His image.

Other things we learn from the example of Christ, as we are sanctified and made more righteous, are some of the attributes mentioned throughout this book. Diligence, humility, patience, honesty, and integrity; these all are things that should define righteous business, but they must define our lives first if they are to define our businesses. Again, we must learn to practice these things. As we work, manage, lead, and do business, we can practice diligence by setting goals. We can practice humility by evaluating our mindset and asking for feedback. We can practice integrity by having an accountability partner. In practicing, we are participating in our personal sanctification, all while contributing to our professional development in righteous business. Though we can learn how to do good business, even relatively ethical business, from books and other leaders, we cannot learn to practice righteous business without looking to the example of Christ.

I appreciate that Solomon put this verse last. Had this verse come first, it may have put us all off the rest of the chapter. Proverbs 12 has been rich with wisdom on how to be righteous and practice righteous business, but it never mentions business. As managers and leaders who are reading this book along with Proverbs 12, we must face the fact that this wonderful wisdom for our businesses was originally written to change the way we conduct our lives. Before we ever change the way we do business, we must change the way we think, the way we speak, and the way we act. Personally, we have to apply what we now know will create a successful business. But we can rejoice in the fact that what we know will create successful business will also create successful life. This path of righteousness is a path of life, a path that does not lead to death.

Before we wrap up our study, it is important to point out that Proverbs 12:28 does not say that if we live righteously, we create a good life for ourselves. It says that life is in this path of righteousness that we are choosing to follow. As we saw in John 15, we cannot create this success or abundance by our own power. Practicing righteousness, we rely on the wisdom, power, and guidance of Christ in us to take our motives and efforts and turn them into something eternally successful.

Am I righteous in my personal life?

In what ways am I unrighteous in my business?

In what ways am I unrighteous in my personal life?

How has my personal righteousness affected my righteousness in business?

CONCLUSION

Righteous Business is good business, but it is hard. Having completed this book, you and I have learned a tremendous amount of what it means to be diligent, humble, honest, and hard working. Proverbs 12 is full of encouragements, challenges, and goals that we can hide within our hearts and minds as we strive for better business practice. In the introduction to this book, I encouraged you to read one chapter each day, treating this book as a devotional. Though what I have written is not profound enough to be devoted to, the holy scripture on which it is based is indeed profound. Please, finish your month of devotion by reading Proverbs 12 in its entirety, appreciating all the wisdom that you have gained over the past month.

The book of Proverbs is full of wisdom that can be applied to our leadership and management. Having finished this book, I challenge you to set a reminder or calendar event on your phone or computer, reminding you to read this book again next year. Instead of reading just in reference to Proverbs 12, the text on which the book is based, look for every chapter and verse of Proverbs that relates to the topics discussed in each chapter. This will undoubtedly take longer than a month to complete, but I believe it will help you deepen your walk with God and your understanding of what it means to be righteous in life and in business. This might even be a way you can lead others in a study of the principles discussed in this book!

Keep this book on your bookshelf, on your nightstand, on your desk, or wherever you can access it quickly and easily! Some of my favorite books on leadership are in this sort of short form writing, consisting of many short chapters on specific topics. I keep my five favorites close by my desk so that whether I am studying, writing, or even working, I can reference them easily. This has been an immense help to me in my personal and professional development as I read and reread chapters pertaining to certain attributes or topics in which I am struggling and growing. In fact, I usually read these same books every single year. It is my hope that you would do the same with this book. Keep it handy, read it often, and let the wisdom of Proverbs 12 soak deep into your heart and mind.

BIBLIOGRAPHY

1) OpenStax. (2019). Principles of Management. OpenStax. https://openstax.org/books/principles-management/pages/1-introduction

2) Segal, Troy. (2021). Enron Scandal: The Fall of a Wall Street Darling. Investopedia. https://www.investopedia.com/updates/enron-scandal-summary/

3) Bolman, Lee & Deal, Terrance. (2017). Reframing Organizations: Artistry, Choice, and Leadership, 6th ed. Jossey-Bass.

4) Mason, Eric. (2013). Manhood Restored: How The Gospel Makes Men Whole. B&H Publishing Group.

5) Sinek, Simon. (2019) The Infinite Game. SinekPartners, LLC.